Antonio of Bethlehem

Samih Masoud

Translated from Arabic
by
Bassam S. Abu-Ghazalah

inner child press, ltd.

Credits

Author
Samih Masoud

Translator
Bassam S. Abu-Ghazalah

Editor
hülya n. yılmaz, Ph.D.

Cover Design & Graphics
Inner Child Press, ltd.

General Information
Antonio of Bethlehem
Author: Samih Masoud

1st Edition: 2020
Published in Arabic in 2020 by Alan Publishers in Amman, Jordan

This publishing is protected under Copyright Law as a "Collection". All rights for all submissions are retained by the individual author and / or artist. No part of this publishing may be reproduced, transferred in any manner without the prior WRITTEN CONSENT of the "Material Owner" or its representative, Inner Child Press, ltd. Any such violation infringes upon the Creative and Intellectual Property of the Owner pursuant to International and Federal Copyright Law. Any queries pertaining to this "Collection" should be addressed to Publisher of Record.

Publisher Information:
Inner Child Press
intouch@innerchildpress.com
www.innerchildpress.com

This Collection is protected under U.S. and International Copyright Laws

Copyright © 2020: Samih Masoud

ISBN-13: 978-1-952081-21-7 (inner child press, ltd.)

$ 24.95

Dedicated to

all those who fight

for the sake of having

the sun of liberty everywhere

Table of Contents

The Author's Introduction   ix

Antonio of Bethlehem

Chapter One	3
Chapter Two	11
Chapter Three	17
Chapter Four	23
Chapter Five	29
Chapter Six	35
Chapter Seven	39
Chapter Eight	45
Chapter Nine	53
Chapter Ten	59
Chapter Eleven	65
Chapter Twelve	73
Chapter Thirteen	81
Chapter Fourteen	87
Chapter Fifteen	93
Chapter Sixteen	99
Chapter Seventeen	105
Chapter Eighteen	111

Table of Contents ... *continued*

Chapter Nineteen	119
Chapter Twenty	125
Chapter Twenty-One	131
Chapter Twenty-Two	137
Chapter Twenty-Three	143
Chapter Twenty-Four	149
Chapter Twenty-Five	157
Chapter Twenty-Six	163
Chapter Twenty-Seven	171
Chapter Twenty-Eight	177
Chapter Twenty-Nine	183
Chapter Thirty	191
Chapter Thirty-One	197
Chapter Thirty-Two	203
Chapter Thirty-Three	209
The Author's Epilogue	*213*

Epilogue 217

About the Author	219
About the Translator	221
Other Books by the Author	225

The Author's Introduction

It was nine o'clock when I left my house in a hot July morning in 1969. It took me about half an hour to get to my work place in the center of Kuwait, where I have been living for several years.

I had just entered my office when the telephone rang. On the other end of the line was my friend Abd al-Fattah, the Egyptian journalist for *al-Hadaf*, a Kuwaiti newspaper. He soon moved the conversation toward politics and gave me the latest developments in Arabic countries. He then asked me, if I would like to meet an important international fighter whom he was going to interview this evening about his experiences. "Yes, by all means!" was my immediate answer.

Abd al-Fattah told me that man's name was Antonio and that he was of Colombian and Palestinian origin. He happened to be visiting one of his relatives in Kuwait. My friend added that he had an extensive history with the resistance movement in Palestine, but also in Cuba and other South American countries.

I asked Abd al-Fattah, if he knew Antonio's relative. "It is Nassri, a friend who has been living in Kuwait for a long time. He is a businessman who owns three shops in Hawalli and al-Nuqra where he sells some Palestinian products." He then added, "I'll come over at six to pick you up, and we shall go together to his home, which is also in Hawalli."

We ended our phone conversation. I was excited about what I had heard from Abd al-Fattah. I was sure that, with his distinguished status as a journalist, he would serve the readers of *al-Hadaf* best in delivering them information about the international scope of a unique resistance movement. His brilliant writings about the problems of the Arabs had after all always a wide-reaching impact on the media when political platforms were concerned.

At six in the evening, Abd al-Fattah came over with his car and we left for his friend's home. In Hawalli, he stopped in front of a building on Ibn Khaldoun Street. We knocked on the door of a flat on the first floor. Nassri opened the door with a lovely smile, and Abd al-Fattah introduced me to him.

In the living room, we met two men whom Nassri introduced to us. They were his relatives, Antonio and Fadhel Rasheed. Both men started talking about events they lived through in Palestine before 1948.

I felt overwhelmed by what I was hearing about the resistance movement. With the words of a veteran fighter, Antonio talked about the lessons learned from the war of June 1967, which had taken place a short while ago. He spoke bitterly:

"It was a major setback. We were robbed of the beauty of life within merely six days. When Arabs suffered a great defeat and their land became largely an occupied territory, all our dreams were destroyed. Everything around us changed in a short period of time, a change that left in me an everlasting sorrow."

Silence prevailed. Antonio then once again spoke with melancholy: "We hope that our efforts will spread and strengthen us against these terrible attacks."

Antonio was sitting beside me. I found him to be very good-natured. He had a resemblance to the Cuban leader Fidel Castro. He was tall, had a thick black beard and was wearing a suit in a striking green color that looked like a military uniform. His big black eyes revealed his Arabic origin. His command of Arabic was impressive. The Palestinian colloquialisms he used showed me his preference for the spoken form.

Antonio's roots traced back to Bethlehem. His grandfather had immigrated to Colombia where he settled down. Under his grandfather's patriotic influence, Antonio visited Palestine several times, having participated in the 1936 Palestinian revolution as well as in the war of 1948. His homeland remained alive in Antonio's heart throughout his family's expatriation. He had dedicated himself to the Palestinian resistance movement, but also always supporting the oppressed in many South American countries. As for his presence here, it provided me with a personal insight into the Palestinian movement at large.

I thought that no other human being could have looked happier than Antonio during his interaction with Nassri. The broad smile he had while looking at him conveyed his feelings about his relative and the strong bond between them. Their connectedness surpassed geographic boundaries and portrayed an incarnated Bethlehem, while it unearthed the city's ancient origin. Their lovely smiles were a reminder of the intimate relationship between the man and the place. That unmistakable link pulled all the dispersed parts of their lives together and reunited a faraway past in the heart of the homeland and a present that was ruled by the shadows of defeat and exile.

The scenes of the past came to life in Antonio's heartfelt words when he related to us the time of his youth and his struggles for Palestine's survival. He delved into the vaults of his memory in a gleaming account of a love for his friend, Fadhel. Antonio was 27 when they fought in several battles together near Jerusalem, the last of which was the

Battle of al-Qastal – deeply engraved into Palestine's modern-day history.

Antonio described fervently the battles that these two friends fought together with the Holy Jihad Army in Jerusalem and its vicinity. He did not omit any details as far as their contact with people and the events they witnessed on Palestinian land.

With a loving glance at Fadhel, Antonio spoke with enthusiasm:

"Let me introduce to you my commander, Fadhel Rasheed with whom I fought in the Battle of al-Qastal near Jerusalem. The sky over that village in that early morning remained dark. Life had not awakened on that sad day after the death of our chief commander. At the time, he had reached the peak of his resistance. Fadhel alone efficiently and courageously proceeded with that battle as planned. All along, he was grieving over our chief commander's martyrdom and the fall of the village of al-Qastal. That village had a strategic location, for it was on the main road between Jerusalem and Jaffa."

Antonio paused, looked around and continued to talk about the critical role Fadhel played in the Rasheed Aali al-Kilani's revolt. That uprising had inflamed Iraq in the 1940s and led to Fadhel's arrest by the British. He then was exiled to

Mauritius, where he was jailed and savagely tortured in the Port Louis Prison.

Antonio described how serious Fadhel's condition was after getting out of that prison and detailed his transfer to Germany to receive medical treatment. Afterward, Fadhel volunteered to fight in Palestine and became an exceptional asset for the al-Jihad al-Muqaddas Forces. After the Palestinian Nakba, he went to Kuwait, where his comrades helped him obtain a prime post in one of the offices of the Kuwaiti Ministry of Finance.

At that moment, the two men looked at each other. Fadhel appeared to be embarrassed about being the center of attention. The word was that he always kept silent about actual events. His unease did not stop us from continuing our conversation. The subject came to the prominent occurrences in Palestine's recent history, particularly those that shaped the state of affairs for Arabs on all levels of their existence.

In his capacity as a journalist, Abd al-Fattah talked about the largely concealed matters from about two years ago, all of which related to the defeat of Arabs in 1967. He then gave Antonio a smile before speaking to him directly:

"It is time for our interview. Let us tell our Kuwaiti readers something about you and your involvement with the international resistance movements."

"I'm ready to answer all your questions in detail", Antonio responded. "I shall share with you the relevant events of the past, my attachment to my homeland and my actions on behalf of the world's oppressed people."

As Antonio talked candidly about the resistance movements in which he participated as a fighter in Cuba, Mexico, Guatemala, Bolivia and Palestine, the interview unraveled the unknown traits of a remarkable international movement.

Abd al-Fattah was posing one question after another, recording everything without taking a break. He seemed as diligent as Antonio to cover all the specifics about the movement in Palestine and the forced departure of Bethlehem's and Ramallah's Palestinian population. Antonio gave a detailed account of his grandfather's immigration from Bethlehem to Colombia about a hundred years ago. He also spoke about his grandfather's lifelong bond to Bethlehem, stressing that he owed his own attachment to Palestine to his grandfather.

Abd al-Fattah seemed utterly excited. He raised more questions, asking Antonio also about his comrades in Cuba. Antonio told him that he met Che Guevara by chance in Bogotá on the 2nd of July in 1952. Ever since that day, they became close friends and their friendship grew despite the laps of time. Antonio had met Fidel Castro through Guevara. He then talked about his involvement with the first group of fighters of the Cuban Revolution. That group had crossed the sea from the Mexican port of Tuxpan to the shores of Cuba on a boat called "Granma". Antonio thus had joined the Battle of Santa Clara that had resulted in a victory for the Cuban revolution.

The interview came to an end at a late hour of the night. Abd al-Fattah thanked Antonio, describing his answers as heartfelt hymns shared in a most sincere way. Then Fadhel began to speak. Everyone listened to his words intently:

"What I've heard from you right now, Antonio, was a true account. You must write your experiences in a book before all the details are forgotten."

Antonio answered humbly in a soft voice: "It's difficult for me to write in Arabic." To that, I replied without wasting any time: "In that case, why don't you record everything to be transcribed into the written form later?" He liked my idea. Fadhel then suggested that I help Antonio with the recording. We decided to meet the next day at Nassri's house to start the process. At the time, we did not know that it was going to take us ten days to complete our work.

The three of us met as planned. Antonio justifiably thought that his life story should start with the time period when his grandfather was still alive. That dear man had after all the most significant impact on Antonio's overall worldview. Besides, it was his grandfather from whom he learned about his Arabic-Palestinian roots and was, thanks to him, able to accumulate unforgettable memories throughout his life. While he was retrieving the past, Antonio trembled.

As I have mentioned earlier, the recording process took us ten days to finish. We met every day for several hours until late at night. Each time, Antonio went through the many passages of his life. All along, he talked in a charming voice and with clear-cut words. His accounts filled 15 tapes. We listened to them several times in order to make sure that the recording was intact and conveyed everything accurately. After our work was done, Fadhel took the tapes so that he could transfer the contents to paper.

Three days later, Fadhel called me with a sad news: Antonio had passed away in his sleep. I was shaken. Antonio was only sixty years old. This loss was tragic also because of his exceptional dedication to the betterment of life in Palestine and South America, but to that of humanity at large.

The next day, a great number of Palestinians, Kuwaitis and other Arabs escorted Antonio's body to his grave at the Christian Cemetery in the al-Sulaibikhat region. His interview was published in *al-Hadaf* only a few days ago. The article described him as an international and Palestinian fighter. The funeral attendees must have been aware of his significance. They seemed to be feeling the void he left behind.

Days had passed, and I continued working in Kuwait. Fadhel left for Iraq, his homeland. He eventually moved to Germany and settled down there. Many years later, I visited Fadhel in the small German town Auckland near Cologne where he was living. We talked about our time in Kuwait and reminisced about our friend Antonio. Fadhel told me how sorry he was for not being able to transcribe Antonio's audio-interview. He had been suffering from poor health. He still had the tapes, though, and they were all intact.

I offered to take the recordings and transform them into text myself, which I have done for this book. Throughout this undertaking, I had to rephrase some of Antonio's colloquial expressions in proper Arabic; however, I have completed that task without encroaching on the essence of his actual accounts.

What follows next is Antonio's own story.

Samih Masoud

Antonio of Bethlehem

Antonio of Bethlehem

Chapter One

Antonio of Bethlehem

Samih Masoud

Shortly after the sunset on a Sunday, I started recording my life story. I looked at my past with all its events that had taken place around me. I have been encouraged to record them as representative offerings in the hope that they would bring me closer to myself, my family and my friends. I wanted my past to surface through my own statements to be read after my death.

Seeing myself inside an open book, the way I was in the past and the way I am now, is highly important to me. I shall follow the essence of my life without stopping until I complete my story. My words will hopefully connect with one another and articulate my memories adequately so that they become an eternal part of me.

I should mention my name right away. I must say that I am proud of it, for it actually embodies many names. I was baptized in one of the churches of Bogotá, the capital of Colombia, as "Antonio Manuel Caro", which was known as my name throughout my college years. My mother had conceived it to fit my Colombian identity. It is the name registered in official papers, before I acquired my Cuban nationality. In fact, I get confused when I say it, trying to make sense of it, because its letters are written in a complicated manner.

My grandfather used to call my name with an Arabic flavor as "Anton Saleem" to confirm my Arabic roots. My father would insist on adding his name by calling me "Anton Jameel Saleem", which aligns with the Hispanic tradition of identifying names in their multifaceted forms. In Guatemala, Mexico and Cuba, I had the name of "Antonio, the Colombian". The name nearest to my heart, however, is "Antonio al-Talhami" – "Antonio of Bethlehem", which I deeply love because it reflects my Palestinian origin and my linkage to Bethlehem, Christ's town of birth and the homeland of my ancestors.

I was born in Bogotá in the last evening of 1909. After having had three girls, my family was happy with the birth of the first son. My father was elated as he was given a son who would help him in his life's endeavors. He tried to convince my mother that her son was the most beautiful baby on Earth.

I wish to visit many memories of my early days in a chronological manner, while I intend to blend them with accounts of events and people as I remember them. I want to mention everyone whom I met, but especially those with whom I had a friendship.

Here I am. After many years, I am knocking on the doors of the past. I open them and am happy to see the light that emerges from them. There is a special place for my grandfather Saleem in my memories. When I think of him, it is as if I can see him in front of me, just the way he had been in real life. He was tall. His moustache was so prominent that it looked like it was covering most of his face. He talked in a deep voice and had distinctive eyes that expressed intelligence and good-heartedness.

I miss him and wish that he could be here to tell me more about his life, like the interesting stories he used to tell us in Spanish, mixing them with Arabic words, especially whenever he talked about his parents and two brothers. His voice trembled whenever he sang sad Palestinian songs, which were accompanied by tears: "Awf, Maiyjana and Dal'ouuna." The melodies would come across as tender and embracing of his life struggles.

I was my grandfather's first grandchild. I was told later on that my birth filled him with immense happiness. He

Samih Masoud

took care of me ever since I was in a cradle. Since the time I began to walk, he spent many hours with me. When I was a baby, he offered me his lap. When I got older, he always wanted me to sit beside him, especially when his friends came over. He would gleefully introduce me to them. I had the chance to accompany him in his travels in Colombia. Among his grandchildren, I was indeed the closest to him, and our family had accepted that distinction with pleasure.

I have many fond memories of my grandfather. Years after his death, they are still strongly etched in me. When I think about him, I feel a mixture of love, sadness and hope. My memories of him are the purest.

I love to reminisce about every moment I spent with my grandfather. I loved his thoughts about life, man and expatriation. I have always wished to be with him, sit next to him the way I used to, and listen to him talk sorrowfully about his past in his city of birth, Bethlehem.

I would sit silently by my grandfather, delighted by the warmth of his presence, especially in those times when he talked about his departure from Bethlehem for another world at a young age. He always longed for Bethlehem and its people. He had many stories about his relatives. Whenever he talked about them, he would let out a sigh, as that was how he expressed his bitterness over their forced exile from his homeland. He used to describe his mother concisely, stressing her big eyes and thick hair. Whenever he talked about her, he would be in tears: "My mother's face was touched by Virgin Mary!"

Antonio of Bethlehem

When the subject was Bethlehem, my grandfather chose his words carefully. There was so much compassion in his eyes during those moments. He would reminisce about Bethlehem with pride in his voice: "In Bethlehem, Jesus Christ was born and all Christians from all parts of the world perform their pilgrimage there. Muslims also consider it a holy town."

He would talk about Bethlehem without a pause, moving from one story to another in his memories of his family, friends and neighbors. Every now and then, I would interrupt him to inquire about some details, which always made him feel excited and happy. Thanks to my grandfather's stories, I was not only well-informed about Bethlehem, but also about Palestine overall as well as other Arabic countries.

I never forget these words: "You do not belong to this place (Colombia). Carve it into your memory that you belong to Bethlehem and Palestine. Your roots trace back to Arabic countries from East to West." He would smile happily upon hearing me repeat his words, then hug me and say enthusiastically: "You are a real Talhami, my child!"

My grandfather was born in the morning of a day in the year 1843 when Palestine was under the Ottoman rule. Turkish was the official language, and educational opportunities were scarce. Therefore, he could seek an education only among the lower classes. He had finished a school that belonged to one of the Christian monasteries. Afterwards, he had joined a trade school.

Samih Masoud

My grandfather had chosen wood carving as his specialization, which was famous in Bethlehem and popular among pilgrims. This profession was related to other craftsmanship, like cutting olive wood and mother of pearls into artistic forms. He was excellent in his trade. He worked in a famous workshop near the Church of the Nativity, supplying merchants with products traditional to Bethlehem. He thus was able to create his art as inspired from the natural environment of his beloved Bethlehem.

Antonio of Bethlehem

Chapter Two

Antonio of Bethlehem

Samih Masoud

With the passage of time, the bond between my grandfather and me grew stronger, and how he lived his life affected me greatly. I remember many things about him vividly, especially his departure from the Palestinian port of Jaffa when he was in his twenties. I always get highly emotional when I think of the details of his journey.

Together with his parents and two brothers, my grandfather had left Bethlehem on a day in July in a carriage and travelled on rugged roads for three days until they finally reached Jaffa. The family then spent two days in the home of my grandfather's uncle who lived in the al-Manshiyya district. It was this uncle who had made all the necessary travel arrangements for my grandfather, including the stamp on his Ottoman passport.

My grandfather noticed how tense and emotionally shaken his parents looked at the time of his departure. Their eyes had become mere holes on their faces, filled with tears, and they were barely able to speak. Whenever he talked about that day, he would utter the same words: "Those moments when I had to shake their trembling hands for a goodbye was the most difficult time in my life. Had it not been for the poor life conditions in Palestine during the Ottoman rule, I would have never left." He then would stop talking for a while to collect himself before he could describe his emotions while leaving Jaffa:

"My heart rate increased as I forced myself to the dock where 'Miss Lydia', the ship, had anchored, with smoke coming out of its chimney. She was an English passenger and cargo ship going to the English Port of Southampton, where, after a brief stop, she was going to sail to the USA. I stood with the rest of the passengers in front of the long footbridge. Less than half an hour later, it was time to move." In a sad voice, my grandfather would continue with his story:

"I stood on the ship's deck waving and saw my folks waving their white handkerchiefs at me. I kept on waving while the ship blew her siren. She then started leaving the harbor slowly, slicing the Mediterranean Sea towards our first destination. Gradually, the land disappeared from sight while I stayed put in my place, looking at the horizon."

My grandfather's facial expressions always revealed the sadness he must have felt while the ship more and more sharpened the divide between his family and himself. While she was navigating on her route, he kept looking at Jaffa although it could no longer be seen. "Finally, giving up, I leaned against an edge on the deck, feeling sad for having to leave my family and home. After a while, I started to interact with the passengers from Palestine who were also seeking to settle down in the USA to look for new life opportunities."

As he would repeat to me, a bit later, he found himself enjoying the high waves that were pounding the ship, causing her to sway. He then wanted to get some sleep in the hope that he might overcome his sadness. Because his ticket was cheap, he had to sleep on the deck. He got himself a mattress and slept among a great number of other passengers. During meal times, they were given food according to the price of their tickets.

My grandfather would always speak up regarding that matter: "On that ship, I learned for the first time what discrimination was."

For a week, he spent his days on the sea in a similar fashion. Then the ship sailed to the English Channel. A part of the cargo was unloaded there. Jaffa oranges made up the majority of it. Another kind of cargo was then loaded to be carried to the USA.

"Miss Lydia" stayed in Southampton for three days. On the fourth day, she set sail towards the Atlantic Ocean.

Many passengers were hit by seasickness. My grandfather also became sick, especially at nighttime. He recovered when the ship docked at a large port on the Atlantic shore.

The trip took 50 days, at the end of which my grandfather left the ship with other Palestinian passengers. The captain announced in English that the ship had reached the American land where their trip had come to its end. As they had known no other language except Arabic, they followed his instructions to leave.

Antonio of Bethlehem

Chapter Three

Antonio of Bethlehem

Samih Masoud

In the morning of September 1st in 1863, my grandfather took his first steps as an immigrant. He had to look for a job. He was assuming that he was in the USA. Eventually, he realized that he was in a small and poor country called Panama that was not worth migrating to. It was a connecting link between two continents – North America and South America. It was distinguished by its location: it stood between two oceans, the Atlantic and the Pacific.

When my grandfather arrived there, the first French attempt to build the Panama Channel had failed, which led to the abandonment of plans to link both oceans. This project was to be materialized many years later with the support of Americans. The new channel was critical because it was going to shorten ships' travel distance. This aspect made it one of the most important projects known.

My grandfather looked always sad when he talked about the time he spent in Panama. He would speak angrily: "Our ship's captain misled us when he announced that we were in the USA. That way, he got rid of the poor passengers and was thus able to replace them with others whose destination was New York, which meant a considerable financial gain for his company."

For an entire week, my grandfather woke up every morning with tears on his pillow as a result of that deception. He would say to me: "That incident was a clear example of man exploiting man. It's one of the crimes committed by white men against others." He would then add: "The English are the most corrupt people on Earth. Their crimes against their colonies should never be forgiven. They are by all means the scum of mankind. Their only goal is to rob the people they colonize and humiliate them."

Antonio of Bethlehem

It took my grandfather some time to find a way to leave Panama. He did not have the money for a ticket to New York. He was panic-stricken. At last, he ran into some of his country men who had accompanied him on "Miss Lydia". From them, he learned that Panama was actually a part of a federation called the United Colombian States where jobs and good living standards were obtainable. Colombia had an intensive agriculture, including the growth of coffee beans. There were also some important gold mines and many other precious metals.

He decided to join ten Palestinians who were going to live in Colombia. They had to go on foot to their promising new country. They had to walk great distances through land and forests on high mountains to reach the southeast of Panama. They moved fast on sunny days and slept in open air throughout the long summer nights.

They first arrived in Córdoba (Qurtuba). They stopped in a village where they met Nazih, an emigrant. He had originally travelled to Colombia from the Biqaa region of Lebanon. He had been living in Córdoba for the last ten years, selling clothes. He was a very friendly man who accommodated them in his nearby farm by a small stream in an open green area.

In their first night, their host told them that the Spanish had given "Cordova" its name after the ancient Arabic city Qurtuba, the city of sciences during Spain's Andalusian era. Nazih gave them also valuable information about the different places and job opportunities in Colombia as well as in other cities, including Bogotá. He talked to them about The Andes, the Nevado del Ruiz volcano near Bogotá and The Amazon River that springs out of The Andes and streams through many countries, including Colombia. He particularly stressed that it was world's largest and second longest river, in which more than 3,000 kinds of fish lived.

Nazih finished his words by saying: "This is your new homeland. It is better to live here than be in the ugly USA. That country was built over the corpses of the original inhabitants and on the slavery of Africans."

My grandfather asked him: "Is it safe to settle down in Colombia?" Nazih confirmed to him that so far it was safe and that there was no indication of a change for the worse in the future. He also advised them not to rush to find a place to live in Colombia, that they should think thoroughly first before making any decisions.

Eventually, they went to sleep. In the morning, they began to explore the area for a proper place to live. They decided to try Cartagena on the Caribbean Sea.

Antonio of Bethlehem

Chapter Four

Antonio of Bethlehem

Samih Masoud

Nazih agreed with them and hailed two carriages to take them to their destination. They thanked him warmly for his hospitality as they bid goodbye in front of his shop. Then they left for Cartagena. It was a major port and thus a touristic landmark in Colombia with Phoenician influences and had a rich history that started with the Spanish colonialization of South America.

As my grandfather arrived in Cartagena, he first noticed the mountains nearby which were covered with dense forests. After getting a job in a big hotel, he decided to settle down near the charming shores. His companions had also found work but elsewhere. One of them, Jameel Izziddeen, had also acquired a job in the same hotel as my grandfather. Jameel came from Abu-Wash, a small village near Ramallah. He was deeply attached to Palestine and loved to talk about it all the time. My grandfather liked and respected him greatly. On their first workday, he said to him with a serious tone in his voice: "Our mother, Palestine, brings us together, my dear Jameel, here and there and everywhere." His friend's response was equally heartfelt: "Yes, Palestine is our mother and you are my brother!"

My grandfather whispered: "This way we can bear everything in our expatriation because we are connected through our mutual homeland."

Time passed slowly in the hotel. My grandfather wanted to learn Spanish. A special course was being offered to new immigrants. Together with Jameel, he started going to a night school, housed in one of the churches. Within a few months, the two friends completed their classes. They were thus able to communicate with people in Spanish. Their incentive pleased the hotel owner who paid them special attention.

Antonio of Bethlehem

Working helped my grandfather ease the severity of his separation from home. He was eager to tell his parents about his new life. He tried to find a way to get in touch with them but was unable to do so back then.

One early morning, my grandfather noticed that something was different on the coast. Looking panicked, people were rushing to higher land, pushing one another. A hurricane was moving towards Cartagena. The hotel was vacated immediately. Torrential rains and gigantic waves were spreading terror over the city's shores as well as the nearby towns and villages.

My grandfather was also panic-stricken. He had uncontrollable spasms and was unable to breathe for a while. Then his heart rate returned to normal.

He told me a lot about his hurricane-fright. A deadly danger had come very close. Afterward, everything around him was different. Cartagena didn't look the same anymore, as the hurricane had left a great devastation behind, including many deaths – not to forget the seriously injured.

On that day, he came to know that hurricanes were common occurrences at the Caribbean shores during their particular seasons. They were, in other words, an inseparable part of life in that area.

When the immediate danger passed, my grandfather was in a state of mind to think over the hurricane matter with great concern. He shared his thoughts with his dear friend, Jameel:

"Mankind is capable of starting wars and revolutions, changing regimes and forcing ideologies upon others, but is helpless against nature. Mankind is weak and cannot stand against nature's destructive powers."

Samih Masoud

Jameel asked him in a low voice: "What are we doing, staying here in this hurricane region?" My grandfather suggested: "Let's move somewhere else!"

An agreement was reached silently between the two friends. They went to the hotel manager to tell him about their decision. He kept quiet for a brief moment, then spoke affectionately: "I wish that you would keep your jobs at the hotel because I see in you both a great potential for success." For a few days, he tried to convince them to stay. When he finally realized that they were determined to leave, he gave them recommendation letters to take along to some of his friends who were businessmen in various cities. One of those letters was addressed to the manager of a famous emerald mine in a village called Mozo by The Andes. The two friends said their goodbyes and thanked the hotel manager warmly for his kindness. He reassured them that they would always be welcome at the hotel, if they were to come back: "I promise to stop all hurricanes!"

All three men laughed and the two friends went over to the carriage station in front of the hotel.

Antonio of Bethlehem

Chapter Five

Antonio of Bethlehem

Samih Masoud

My grandfather and Jameel rode on a big carriage to The Andes, leaving behind them their good-hearted hotel manager Pablo.

As they started to move up the hill, they looked at the Caribbean Sea for one last time. The carriage took a winding road through thick forests over high mountain slopes.

The journey was fine at the beginning. But then they ended up on rough roads while going up the mountain. My grandfather told me that the carriage was shaking and swerving when the wheels were hit by water running down from the mountain passes. He also described to me how much the horses were suffering. He knew that their hoofs were hurting, as they neighed after each pound on the ground, sending a loud echo into the silence of the night. As for the driver, he was merciless whipping their backs and yelling at them whenever they slowed down. The horses were in bad shape, panting the entire time.

My grandfather always calmly continued with his story about that time in his life. He would add other details to it, as those memories were engraved deeply in him. He particularly was adamant about telling me how they slept on muddy ground in the middle of wilderness with all kinds of wild animals howling nearby.

Five days later, they reached the west of the Boyoka region on the east of The Andes. The area had an abundance of rivers and lakes as well as emerald mines. They passed through a few villages until they arrived in Mozo, the village near Tonkha – the capital of Boyoka.

The two young men left the carriage and immediately went to the emerald mine where they delivered Pablo's recommendation letter to the manager. He was amused: "You ran away from the hurricanes to this area which is covered with heavy snow for a long time for most of the year!"

Jameel's answer was ready: "We can wear warm clothes and have fire at home all the time; but hurricanes cause people to die."

The manager nodded his head in agreement. He seemed happy to see that these two young men spoke Spanish fluently. He told them about available posts and their sleeping arrangements. He introduced them to his assistant. The two friends read the work requirements and thanked the manager for his help. He informed them about the significance of this mine, one of the largest in Colombia and well-known for the quality of its emerald stones. The original inhabitants had excavated such stones hundreds of years ago. After the Spanish occupied Colombia, they found out about the mines and extracted from them large amounts of rare emerald stones, making Spain wealthy.

The assistant manager then took them to their barracks close to the mine where all workers slept. He gave each of them a cot made of tree branches. He instructed them about the rotational sleep schedule, which was set according to the time of work in the mine.

All cots were covered with straw, finely braided in the indigenous way. The straw was supposed to be good to protect against the severe cold of the mountains. The two friends were surprised to hear that the workers had to do the repair themselves when they had broken straws in their cots.

In their first night in the barracks, my grandfather and Jameel met a number of mineworkers who belonged to the original inhabitants of America, the Mokaná, the Kimbaya and the Tairona. The two friends communicated with them in Spanish, their ancestors' tongue.

Samih Masoud

One of them, Edwin, talked about the political history of Colombia, the ongoing violence in the country and the injustice against the marginal population. A few others criticized the political conditions in Colombia, showing their support for the organized resistance by the working class, while they stressed the need to change the world into a more just and humanitarian one.

Discussions with Edwin and his colleagues occurred regularly. So, my grandfather and Jameel understood the extent of the discrimination suffered by the original inhabitants and the Africans in all walks of life very well. They also learned about some other dark sides of life as far as poverty, starvation and oppression.

Edwin was happy talking about the end of slavery in Colombia in 1851, but added in a sad voice: "Slavery was eliminated officially, but it is still practiced today in different forms, as we see it being revived by businessmen and mine owners. That it is so is obvious when one looks at our low wages and poor working conditions in dark tunnels below the ground."

My grandfather and Jameel decided to join the secret union of the mine workers. The union's main goal was to defend the rights of its members and have their wages increased and their work conditions improved. Thus, the two friends became a part of their first resistance movement in Colombia.

Antonio of Bethlehem

Chapter Six

Antonio of Bethlehem

Samih Masoud

The mine became my grandfather's refuge where the sound of his footsteps became well-known as he moved swiftly through the many tunnels, touching the iron cables on the ground along the way. He would excavate the rocks with a heavy hammer from early morning till sunset. He received only a small wage, not equaling his efforts or the dangers he was facing deep under the ground.

One evening, my grandfather and Edwin went to the café which mine workers attended. They sat in a corner with a view of the forest. My grandfather's imagination took the scene to the eastern part of The Andes. Suddenly, an explosion shook the entire area. Edwin suspected it to come from the mine.

My grandfather shouted in panic that Jameel was in the mine for his night shift. They rushed to the main entry of the mine. A crowd of mineworkers had gathered there, all looked stricken with anxiety. Soon, the administration issued an announcement: a large number of explosives had become active inside the mine for unknown reasons, the tunnels were blocked by rocks and dirt and many mine workers were still inside.

Efforts for saving the workers continued for a long time amid toxic gases.

My grandfather was highly worried about Jameel, and started shouting at the bosses, "Where is my brother, Jameel Izziddeen?"

The bosses kept quiet as he looked at them with anger. Their silence was about to kill him. The next morning, a detailed statement was issued about the incident. Jameel's name was mentioned among those who had lost their lives.

My grandfather angrily yelled at the man who was reading the report. He cursed the owners of the mine and called them brutal killers. He then lost consciousness and fell to the ground. Edwin picked him up and hugged him. When my grandfather was strong enough to stand on his feet, Edwin took him to the barracks. The rest of the workers were crying for their comrades' fate.

For a long time, my grandfather was unable to utter a single word. He was deeply saddened by Jameel's death. Eventually, he collected himself and expressed his sorrow in front of the men he had befriended there, the original inhabitants of the land and the Africans. Jameel of Palestine who travelled with him all this way, was living no longer. My grandfather's eyes were blood-shot and full of tears.

His comrades raised their voices as they criticized the mine owners for failing to provide safety for their workers.

Chapter Seven

Antonio of Bethlehem

As time passed, my grandfather's sorrow increased. His behavior changed. He felt imprisoned inside the tunnels. He resigned from his work, telling the bosses how difficult it was for him to work in a place where his beloved friend, Jameel, was buried. He still felt sad for having to part from Edwin and his other co-workers. He was close to tears when he left.

That part of my grandfather's work life had ended painfully in the mine under the wreckage that killed Jameel. It was a period of time that stayed in his memory throughout his years in Colombia.

Later on, my grandfather decided to move to the Pacific Ocean to look for a job in the coastal regions. He had heard that certain areas were distinguished from others in terms of the weather conditions. This decision brought him to Biona Fontura, a coastal city southwest of Bogotá with a big harbor. However, he stayed there only for a few hours, when he found out that people there were planting coca and dealing with narcotics.

He went to Bogotá instead, where he arrived in a spring morning after a long time on the road. He was very tired. So, he quickly checked in to a small hotel in the southern part of the city – the poor section. He then went to the city center to look for a job.

He had arrived at the time of Barranquilla Carnaval. He was dazzled by the sight of the celebrations, the decorated streets and gardens and the beautiful birds in those gardens.

Antonio of Bethlehem

My grandfather particularly loved the statue of Simon Bolivar in the middle of the city. A big crowd was standing in front of that memorial. He read the words engraved below the statue and realized that Bolivar was a remarkable man who was able to liberate several countries in Middle America (Meso-America) from the Spanish colonialists.

He felt sad for not having a similar, historically significant Arabic hero who would fight to liberate all Arab countries, unifying them, just like what Simon Bolivar, the first president of the Great United Colombian States, had done. Those states were composed of Colombia, Venezuela, Panama, Ecuador and the Grenadine Islands. Those countries had joined each other and formed the Spanish Crown's lands of New Granada with Bogotá as the capital.

My grandfather kept roaming through Bogotá for a month, realizing how large the city was. He observed that many different people with different religions and nationalities lived there. Bogotá was situated by a high mountain, Monserrate. He saw in a tourist brochure that it was the third highest-altitude city in the world, after La Paz and Quito. Because of its location, it was called the "Stars' Neighbor."

One day, my grandfather decided to go up to the top of Monserrate by The Andes. When he reached it, he could see the city in all directions. He thought of the description in the brochure. In it, Monserrate was characterized as being iridescent and full of life, from whose peaks visitors enjoyed the beautiful panorama of the charming Bogotá.

He was witnessing it all. In the distance, he recognized the tracks of world's first tramway with its engine pulled by mules over a wooden railway and its route in the city. He spotted Plaza de Bolivar and the historical Justice Palace as well as the city's oldest museum. He could clearly identify the different city sections: the north, where rich people lived in stately houses; the south, where the majority of the city's residents – namely, the poor, lived.

Antonio of Bethlehem

Chapter

Eight

Antonio of Bethlehem

Samih Masoud

As my grandfather was walking in the Plaza de Bolivar one day, he took a wide street that branched out from the plaza. He was stunned by the sight of the jewelry shops that were filled with marvelous works of green emerald. He stopped in front of an atelier where emeralds were being cut and polished, producing many shapes and sizes, but still being taken from the natural environment and daily life.

He entered that shop and saluted an old man who was sitting in front of an old machine, manually cutting emeralds. He was working the machine by pressing his foot on a pedal. Near that old man were four employees doing the same.

My grandfather introduced himself, upon which the old man welcomed him and told him his name, Ramon. He was the shop owner. My grandfather said to him:

"I know this machine very well and I can adjust it to work faster." Ramon asked him: "Where did you get to know it?" "In Bethlehem," my grandfather replied. The old man spoke with admiration: "Oh, the city of Jesus Christ!" My grandfather nodded his head in agreement and started telling him about his experience in cutting and polishing oysters in a big shop near the Church of Nativity. He added that he was using the same machines and knew their maintenance process very well, but also how to increase their speed.

Ramon said to him: "I am sick now and I need an assistant to keep up with the shop."

Ramon gave my grandfather a trial period of about three months before he could start working there officially. During that time, my grandfather made changes on the machines that improved their capacity and production. After the trial period, the old man offered my grandfather a job with a good salary. Later, my grandfather became the shop's manager.

Antonio of Bethlehem

Ramon stopped working because of his old age. He was content with sitting behind a desk, supervising the sale of his products to the jewelry shops around the city. He was happy talking to my grandfather and listening to him talk about Bethlehem. He was not interested in the spiritual sides of the city alone. He took interest also in the politics behind the Zionist plans my grandfather was well-informed with, being in a position to show historical evidence that Palestine was the land of Arabs.

My grandfather and Ramon developed a close relationship, so much so that he considered Ramon as his new father. He also became active in the labor union activities in Bogotá and spread his thoughts about Palestine to many of his co-workers. He had, after all, always stood against Western colonialism that exploited weak countries.

One day in Easter, Ramon invited my grandfather to have dinner in his home. Accepting the kind invitation, my grandfather bought for the occasion a bouquet of flowers and a box of Spanish sweets, composed of almonds made the Andalusian way. A young pretty girl opened the door. They both introduced themselves to one another. It was Carmen, Ramon's daughter.

My grandfather went inside through a long hallway that ended in a room with traditional furniture. There, he met Ramon and his wife. He realized that he was the only guest and that Carmen was Ramon's only daughter.

Ramon's wife was keen to ask about the feasts in Bethlehem, and my grandfather answered with a lovely memory about his life back home. He felt that Carmen was happy listening to him, and he, in turn, asked Carmen about her childhood. She answered him in a soft voice, while her mother added some more information. In a short amount of time, my grandfather felt highly attached to Carmen.

Carmen volunteered to show Bogotá to my grandfather, knowing that he was still new in the city. My grandfather welcomed Carmen's offer enthusiastically, and they agreed to meet the next morning. She picked him up with her car and took him to different city parts. At Plaza de Bolivar, they stopped and went to a café where they had sugarcane juice that was famous in Bogotá.

My grandfather and Carmen continued to meet. They visited the old city together and viewed its old houses, built in the Andalusian architectural style. They inquired about restaurants and popular workshops. They also went to the top of Monserrate.

My grandfather told Carmen about his beloved hometown Bethlehem, and she listened to him with great interest. As time passed, they began to become more attached to each other. One day, they were sitting at one of the cafés in the old city, when my grandfather took Carmen's hand and asked her: "Would you marry me?"

Unable to answer right away, she trembled and nodded her head in agreement; all along, showing her excitement about my grandfather's question.

Ramon and his wife blessed my grandfather's and Carmen's wish to get married and set a date for the wedding.

One evening, when the moon light was filling Bogotá and The Andes, Ramon arranged a gathering in his garden for the couple. My grandfather had invited ten of his Arabic friends from Palestine, Syria and Lebanon who had settled down in Colombia before him.

In that celebratory gathering, my grandfather and his Arabic friends emotionally sang some popular Arabic songs,

Antonio of Bethlehem

like the Maijana and the Dal'ouna and danced the famous Dabka using a shabbaba made of cane.

The wedding party ended with the sunrise. My grandfather always described that time in an utmost emotional manner.

One year later, my grandfather had his first son, Jameel, named after his dear friend Jameel Abu-Izziddeen from the village of Abu-Qash, who was killed in the mine explosion where they had worked together. Later, my grandfather had two more sons who started working with him in the atelier. When Jameel turned twenty, he was married to Sandra, a girl of Spanish origin. I was born two years later, and my mother insisted on calling me "Antonio" after the name of her brother who died at a young age. After me, my parents had three daughters.

My grandfather was very happy having his first grandchild. He always repeated a saying: "The grandchild is more loved than the son."

I grew up listening with great pleasure to my grandfather talking about his memories of Bethlehem and Palestine in his beautiful voice accompanied by animated hand movements. His stories were a chain of information for me as the political life and social life blended with one another beautifully within a faraway geography.

He told me much about imperialism and the necessity to fight against it wherever it was found, especially in Palestine where the British imperialism had imposed the Jewish immigrants upon the country.

My grandfather used to repeat the rights of the working class and his membership in a labor union that was against the Colombian regime. He talked about his comrades in the union, especially his friend Edwin. He would show me his red card, proving his membership, saying with great confidence: "Look, this card proves that I belong to a secret labor union that works against capitalism." He would then ask me to read what was written on the card, asking me to follow his footsteps and be always on the side of the oppressed to stand against the oppressor.

I always gave him my promise that I would heed his path, also regarding Palestine. For my grandfather used to say to me: "I want you to keep Palestine in your heart at all times." Listening to his heartfelt words, I would raise my right hand and announce my conviction: "I do promise you, Grandfather!"

Antonio of Bethlehem

Chapter

Nine

Antonio of Bethlehem

Samih Masoud

My grandfather was proud of his mother tongue. He had always saw Arabic as the essence of his identity. He tried to teach Arabic to his offspring. However, his attempts were not successful. He was able to teach us some words which we used in our daily life, but even that with difficulty.

He insisted on using the Spanish greeting word "hula" in its Arabic form, "hale", reminding us of the Arabic language within Spain and the impact it had on Spanish as spoken in Colombia and most other South American countries. He told us that the Cashtali language was written in Arabic letters at the time of the Andalusians.

I heard him many times relating with his deep voice some interesting stories from the Andalusian era. I could easily see his enthusiasm whenever he spoke about the boom of Arabic sciences in Cordova. He loved talking about that in a way that would stir emotions in his listeners.

My grandfather was well-spoken. He used to give every subject its worth as he would calmly speak about the past referring to the books he had studied. It was a big surprise to me to hear about the many books which proved that the Andalusian Arabs had discovered America 200 years before Christopher Columbus. He never had any doubt about what had been written in those books.

I was in awe with my grandfather's personality. When I was ready to choose my field in college, I sought his opinion. His immediate suggestion was for me to study political history. He would justify his choice with a reference to Palestine, a land which needed historical and cultural evidencing as far as its Arabic origin in a refusal of the Zionist claim over the land.

Without hesitation, I decided to study political history at St. Thomas University, the oldest university in

Antonio of Bethlehem

Bogotá. My grandfather kept up with my college education with great interest. He was happy to know that I was keeping a keen eye on the Palestinian affairs, condemning the British colonialism and Zionism and refusing adamantly the Balfour Declaration during WWI which had called for the establishment of a Jewish national home in Palestine.

With time, I became involved in student activities. I brought attention to the Palestinian struggle amid the Colombian and other South American matters, stressing the uniting aspects of the freedom fighters, stressing the need to encounter colonialism wherever it was found, because it was against all humanity.

One day, I was invited by the student union president to give a talk on the British imperialist case in Palestine: "How can we find someone better than you to inform us about this subject?"

I told him that my grandfather, Saleem, was much more learned on this subject, because he was born in Palestine and he followed the news every morning and night ever since he stepped foot on Colombian soil. He agreed.

I took the letter of invitation to my grandfather, wondering about his reaction. His response was: "This is the least I can do for my people and my homeland!"

On the day of the lecture, I accompanied my grandfather to the university. We walked together to the designated hall which was completely full. My grandfather was dressed in the traditional Palestinian attire: a qumbaz with blue edges and a white kufiyya (the Palestinian traditional head dress) fastened with a black iqal. The kufiyya at that time was a symbol of the resistance against the British Mandate in Palestine and the deportations imposed by the Jewish forces and their gangs upon Palestinians.

With his tall body, his unusual outfit and his cane, my grandfather had the students' full attention while he walked his way through to his place up front. Students, who may have thought that he had come from another world, saluted him warmly. He took the platform with a lovely smile on his face. Full silence ruled while my grandfather took his time to look at the students first. He then started his talk about his homeland, Palestine, and how he had to leave it, yet always carrying it in his heart.

He started his lecture stating that Palestine was a land of the Arabs and that the Jews had no right in settling there. He referred to a range of thoughts and books on the subject. He talked about the spiritual dimension of the Holy Land which he described as God's paradise on Earth. Different time periods and places were mentioned in his lecture. He talked about Palestine's being a sacred place for all the three major religions. I noticed how peaceful he looked in his accounts of the interaction among its people, irrespective of their beliefs. He expressed his great resentment toward the European countries and the USA for supporting Zionism. As he emphasized, they had strengthened the Jewish presence in Palestine based on some ridiculous claims that they had the right to own the country.

The political and historical dimensions of my grandfather's lecture were well received. Students seemed to lend particular attention to his depiction of the British alliance with the Zionist movement – an alliance that was intensified with the Balfour Declaration and the British Mandate. My grandfather stressed emphatically that this alliance presented a great challenge to Palestine's Arabs, as it confronted them with the British imperialism.

My grandfather paused for a while before resuming his lecture: "These are facts that cannot be refuted. I am sure that a revolt against the British imperialism in Palestine will materialize soon." With those words, my grandfather concluded his lecture. The students applauded him enthusiastically.

He was pleased to answer the many questions that followed his lecture. Afterward, the students gathered around him and followed him to the front entry of the university. Comments and questions continued taking place there. Each time, my grandfather responded energetically.

Whenever I reminisce about his calm voice and the information he delivered on that day, I love him even more. He was my real hero. My most important task had always been to take care of him in his old age.

Chapter

Ten

Antonio of Bethlehem

Samih Masoud

My college years passed by quickly. At the end of each year, I found myself to be different from before. My knowledge had expanded from the books I studied, but also through my active participation in college events. As for the Colombian society, it had a big influence on my overall worldview. My status at the student union had also changed: I was elected as a prominent member of the management. I also joined the Socialist Party. All these new engagements left their impact on me as far as my entire life.

I was proud to stand in front of my grandfather, telling him about the changes in me. Looking at me affectionately, he encouraged me to be on the side of the oppressed and those who fight for the good of humanity. He would spend hours explaining in detail everything related to the humanitarian unity and repeat his favorite phrase that 'oppression was nothing but a threat to humanity wherever it was found in the world'.

I learned from my grandfather not to resort to any sidetracks in my public speeches but to boldly say the truth – even if such was against myself – and to embrace the voice of human justice and the struggle to make it happen. That voice, after all, is an eternal reminder never to die in the hands of time. For injustice of man against man will never stop. It will remain as long as man remains on Earth.

During my studies, I participated in numerous activities inside and outside the university, as I have mentioned earlier. These activities included demonstrations that were called for as a response to some local political developments to refuse the regime's oppressive tendencies against democratic values. I also took part in some required research. At the beginning of my third college year, I was asked to research the political history of a country outside South America. I chose Palestine and defined my subject as the Balfour Declaration that the British issued to create a Jewish homeland in Palestine.

In my research paper, I put down all the information related to that declaration. Out of my nationalist view, I mentioned examples of the Palestinian struggle against that decree and the oppressive British policy that created complicated conditions for Palestinians. I compiled all my findings with passionate words, as I wanted to demonstrate clearly the particular case of Palestine.

I highlighted the Palestinian national movement against the British Mandate and its use of armed resistance against the Jewish emigration to Palestine, a forced move that gave rise to bloody disturbances as early as 1921. Within the same context, I prepared another research on the Sykes-Picot Agreement that ordered the division of the Fertile Crescent between two colonial powers, Britain and France. According to that pact, the Arabic East was drastically altered to the extent that it was divided into smaller states, which made unification prospects difficult, if not impossible.

By the end of my fourth year in college, I completed the required research. A celebration for the graduates took place in one of the large halls of the university. My grandfather, my parents and my sisters attended this ceremony. The university president opened the celebration. The deans of designated colleges then said a few words on behalf of themselves and the graduates. I was chosen to deliver a speech on behalf of the graduating student body of the College of Human Studies.

Samih Masoud

My speech was in line with the mission of my college, but also included my thoughts against imperialism and the policy of the Colombian state in its reactionary position that had caused disastrous results. My doing so led to a month-long investigation by the intelligence service. My file was seen by the interrogators so many times that their questions were utterly familiar to me. This experience helped me discover the horrific interrogation system, a venue that pressured people in order to protect the oppressive regime which was overtly encroaching on human dignity.

Hence was the case of my country of birth, Colombia during my university studies. It was a dreadful time when masses of people lived in the darkness of oppression and despotism. I was shocked by this harsh reality and decided once again to stay true to my principles and resist at all times all rotten regimes in all of South America, even if it meant risking my life for the sake of unity in our continent.

During that period of my life, I understood the meaning of a united South America. In my mind, the image of the needed unity became clearer and clearer by each passing day. It was direly necessary to make it possible in order to achieve dignity for the oppressed classes.

Antonio of Bethlehem

Chapter

Eleven

Antonio of Bethlehem

Samih Masoud

I graduated from the university a few days after turning 24. My grandfather was utterly excited about my diploma and celebrated the occasion with a special gathering to which he invited some of his friends. One friend from Bethlehem sang beautiful Arabic songs and delicious dishes and sweets my grandmother had prepared were served. During dinner, people joyfully talked about various subjects related to Colombia and Palestine. Everyone stayed until midnight, enjoying the entire atmosphere.

After my graduation, my grandfather and I became even closer. We used to stay up late into the night, taking delight in our conversations. Sometimes, we would walk in the streets of Bogotá or sit at one of the cafés in the town center. I felt that I was always in need of his company and listen to his life experiences as a source of immense pleasure.

My grandfather advised me to take up teaching as a profession, for it was important to raise the new generation. When I agreed, he helped me with my application to the specific department for a job in public schools. Luckily, I was accepted.

I received the job offer from a school in the city of Parankia on the Caribbean shore in the northern part of Colombia. Most of its residents are of Red Indian origin, with many others being of African roots. It is considered the first city that was built by the Spaniards in Colombia. What is more important is the fact that it was important for the legendary leader, Simon Bolivar.

One day, when the beginning of the scholastic year was near, my family bombarded me with suggestions. Compassionate recommendations came at me in an attempt to make matters easier for me while I was going to be away from home. Only my grandfather restrained himself. He solemnly repeated only one sentence: "I want you to take care of the poor Indian and African people."

With merely a few words, my grandfather was thus reminding me of the dire need for solidarity with the oppressed. He was also pointing to the opportunity I would now have to effectuate a radical change in the living conditions of the oppressed and in their higher consciousness through my teaching position. He was troubled by one of his most prominent memories, though: the Caribbean hurricanes in Carthage where he had lived one time. As he talked about that place, he brought my attention to nature's dangers and how careful I must be when they take place at the shore where I was going.

My family still had many things to reminisce about when the various stages of my life were concerned. Memories related to Colombia and Palestine, in particular, were emphatically re-visited.

A few days later, I was ready to leave for my workplace. I felt sad for having to say goodbye to my family.

It was a rainy day when I went to the bus station and took the bus to Parankia. The road ran through wide green fields and several towns, including Cartaj and Santa Martha. Santa Martha was famous with its banana export. My grandfather had told me that an Arabic family owned the largest banana farm there.

Eventually, the bus arrived at my destination. After exiting the bus, I immediately went to the Department of Education. There, I met an officer called Mario, who helped me finish all the necessary procedures to start teaching. He then helped me find a house near the school.

I was lucky to be in Parankia at the time of its annual festival. This festival is considered the second largest in the world, where dancing and musical performances take place. The streets are decorated with lovely flowers. The participants wear clothes in bright colors, mostly from an old Colombian tradition. I felt very happy because my new town was distinguished through its artistic flair and endless delightful evenings on the Caribbean shore.

I was busy for a few days getting acquainted with Parankia. My feet were taking me from one street to another, while I was filled with awe at the vast expansion of the town. I was sure that I was in the right place in a traditional city. I discovered also that its residents were kind and, with time, I became friends with many of them.

Ten days later, the new school year started. In the morning, I walked to the school and met the headmaster and a few teachers. Then, I went to the last class of the day and gave an extra-curricular lesson on history. I talked about the original people of South America. I especially enjoyed the fact that the majority of my pupils were Red Indians, the original inhabitants of Colombia. I told them that I was against oppression and against people who supported oppressors.

I talked about the Maya, the Aztec and the Anka in the Middle and South America and the fact that they were at the peak of their civilizations when the Spanish invaded their lands at the beginning of the 16th century. I explained that the roots of those cultures were strong and constituted the foundation of the human civilization at large. I also showed through an analysis of today's most important reminders the achievements of those cultures.

During my lecture, I made sure to stress the spiritual side of those civilizations and their value systems, traditions, norms and beliefs. In a confident voice, I informed my class about the political organization of the Anka with regard to their public land ownership law to secure a life for their people. I gave examples of some of the structures those cultural entities had left behind, such as architectural artifacts and the mountain bridges made out of grape and willow branches, woven with ropes.

I noticed how excited the pupils looked while they listened to the information I presented to them. All of it took them back to their roots. I decided to offer more of those extra-curricular lessons, as I could easily observe the psychological effect this one had on my pupils.

I prepared other class materials that revealed the cultural wealth of the original inhabitants before the arrival of Columbus in their land. I made sure to add an objective that suited the curriculum. In one of my lessons, I raised awareness for the significance of parliamentary democracy as invented by Decanawida, a leader in the 15th century. I taught my pupils that he is considered the founder of the said political system as far as human history and that he created power for the league of the Airokwas nations, thanks to which five Indian tribes at the Great Lakes had been united. The successful experimentation with this league was considered one of the most effective in modern democracies with regard to equality in modern society.

To define the Airokwas' accomplishments more succinctly, I explained to my pupils some facts about Benjamin Franklin, the American. As one of the most notable founders of the United States, he had confirmed that the democracy people enjoyed under that league was unknown in Europe back then. A group of historians and writers in the West had maintained the conviction that such a model, indeed, comprised a real application of democracy based on people's decisions.

On that day, I ended my lesson with what the American historian, Howard Zen, had said about the Airokwas: "The European colonialist stole from the Red Indians their land, civilization and values. He was successful in annihilating them and forced whoever was left to exile to protectorates under their rule. In fact, territories had been created specially to isolate them, distancing them also from natural life. They were forced to live in areas that confronted them with very difficult and inhumane conditions." Howard Zen's conclusions were underlining the fact that the Airokwas, as with other indigenous civilizations, became strangers in their own land after having been forced to protectorates that had a rich and extensive history of oppression and mass annihilation.

Having said these words, I examined the faces of my pupils. I noticed that one of them was gazing at me. So, I asked him: "Do you have a question about today's lesson?" He moved in his seat before answering me: "Have you visited those territories?" I answered him honestly: "I have not visited any protectorate yet, but I have read much about them." I then repeated the key aspects of my lesson and repeated one more time my learned estimation of the conditions back then: unbearable. For the inhabitants had suffered pains to the extent that they were unable to endure life. I talked emotionally about the psychological complexities that increased in the protectorates, leading to many social abnormalities that were not known within the Indian traditions.

I asked my pupils to reflect on this topic. Their points of view led me to the following conclusion: their ancestors' life in the protectorates embodied a kind of old tragedy that had been part of the Elizabethan theatre for a long time, being keen on demonstrating the dramatic developments of many human tragedies.

I had to point out that life in the protectorates was a real, unimagined tragedy – a tragedy for the original inhabitants of the United States and Canada. It was a human tragedy that had been restaged worldwide for hundreds of years in countries that had once lived with pride in their freedom, their democracy and their humane value system.

Chapter Twelve

Antonio of Bethlehem

Samih Masoud

It was not my intention to mention here all the lessons I taught outside the curriculum. What I wanted to show was that those classes helped tighten my relationship with my students and gave me a special popularity among them. That input encouraged me to meet a group of them outside school hours to talk to them privately about the socialist party. Their responses were positive. As time passed by, they expressed their wish to join my party, and eventually, they became my comrades in the resistance movement.

In addition to this initiative within the realm of my teaching responsibilities, I was engaged in another activity. That one prompted emotions and memories, taking me to another world I had not thought of before: writing – writing essays in leftist papers under a pseudonym, that is. I started to contribute to those publications with my writings on various subjects, articulating my convictions against capitalism and the American hegemony over South American countries.

In my articles, I focused on the criminal activity of American institutions toward South American countries and on the extraordinary profits the American monopoly made through a pillage of the natural wealth of those nations, abusing the labor forces and devastating the people. I also wrote about the oppressive regimes that depended on economic pressure, fear tactics, armed reactionary forces and dictatorial agendas to stand against national liberation movements.

My readership grew. An extensive article I had written on the revolutionary leader Simon Bolivar brought me close to him. In that piece, I showed the many attributes of his personality, leadership capacity as well as his vital role in resistance movements. I highlighted the critical details of his famous revolution against Spanish colonialism that had taken over the majority of the South American countries. I resorted to an enlightening observation of Bolivar's most important accomplishments. Freedom for some of the countries was achieved. He had also succeeded in establishing the United States of Colombia. Another concrete outcome of his efforts was the distribution of occupied lands among farmers, along with a ban of wage-free labor and tax payments to the nobles.

    I stressed the need for the national movements to heed the Bolivarian experience and its connection to other liberation initiatives as witnessed throughout the history of South America. My purpose was to direct the attention of my readers to the integral aspects of those undertakings and accomplishments. I wanted to encourage them to consider the possibility of following those reformation paths on an intellectual as well as practical level.

    The reader will not find it strange that, despite my use of pseudonyms in my articles, the intelligence service knew who wrote them. I was taken in for interrogation that lasted ten days. During that time, I had to stop working. I denied all the accusations and refused to sign the papers that were incriminating me. Actually, I ignored the interrogators who had gathered around me and watched me with suspicion.

    I fell into deep thoughts during the last interrogation as I looked with tired eyes around the interrogation room. The momentary calm was interrupted by the chief investigator who said out loud how much he always despised all leftist thought. He repeated his words in a threatening manner. He then let me go because he was unable to find enough evidence to prove his accusations against me.

Samih Masoud

The next day after the interrogations, I received a letter from my grandfather telling me that a protest, organized by the nationalist movement, had taken place in Palestine. The protestors called for an end to the Jewish emigration and the plundering of Arabic lands by Zionists and demanded the formation of a national government to answer to an elected legislative council.

In his letter, my grandfather mentioned that the protest was a great success for the Palestinians. It raised hopes, as this initiative was a part of the Arab Nationalist Movement at large. It also showed that the historical vision of the Arab liberation movement to unify the Arabic lands and to free all Arabic countries from the hegemony of the imperialist forces was very much intact.

The protests continued for six months. After they stopped, I received another letter from my grandfather. This time, he was telling me about the outbreak of a great revolt in Palestine that started to spread throughout all Palestinian cities and villages. In his letter, my grandfather was asking me to prepare myself to participate in the said revolt for the sake of defending the land of our fathers and grandfathers.

Under the nationalist leadership, Palestinians had resorted to an armed revolt to stop the Jewish emigration that was encouraged by the British imperialists, safeguard the Arabs of Palestine, announce independence, establish a democratic Palestinian state on Palestinian soil and fight against the division of Palestine which Britain wanted to apply by force.

I received another emotional letter from my grandfather. In that one, he shared with me his feelings and thoughts about his homeland, along with his immense happiness about the Palestinian revolt. He reassured me that,

Antonio of Bethlehem

had it not been for his old age, he would have joined that resistance movement. In his letter, he also reminisced to me about his time with his family in Bethlehem.

Time went by slowly at the end of the scholastic year. As I was delivering the last lessons, I found enough time to keep up with the latest news on the Palestinian revolution. I also had the chance to get to know the connections to the families and other kinship of my people in Palestine. Wars were in line with my beliefs and interests when all kinds of oppression and colonialism were taken into consideration.

I enjoyed reading my grandfather's letters again and again and seriously considered his suggestion for me to join the Palestinian revolt. I was inspired by his encouragement to be involved in a real struggle for a better world where the people of Palestine would enjoy liberty and dignity. So, I found myself emotionally accepting my grandfather's request. I resigned from my job after my third year of teaching, and requested that my resignation would be effective as of the end of the school year.

I discovered some hidden yearnings inside me that were in harmony with my thoughts. I realized that I was excited about the opportunity to free myself from the confinement of a job routine and to be open to spaces that were full of life. Besides, I had always dreamt of connecting to people within the dimensions of an absolute time and a space. In my new way of existence, I was going to be able to encounter the difficult living conditions of people and help them change their circumstances for the better so that they could reclaim their dignity.

Samih Masoud

One month after presenting my resignation, the school year ended. I thus embarked on a new phase in my life. My days were filled with changes that took away all the chains of a defined job, chains that have been overwhelming me and preventing me from performing my political and intellectual duties toward the goals of my party.

The school was closed, and the moment of goodbyes had arrived. I bid farewell to my colleagues and students, shaking hands with all of them. I then rushed to the bus station and took the bus to Bogotá.

Antonio of Bethlehem

Chapter Thirteen

Antonio of Bethlehem

A day later, I arrived in Bogotá in the evening and went to the western side of the city where my family lived. I became highly emotional when I saw my grandfather, my parents and the rest of my family.

My grandfather's question broke the silence. He was asking me, if I had read his letters. "Yes!" I answered, "I read them all with utmost attention." After a brief moment, he wondered out loud: "Do you accept my suggestion to go to Palestine to join the revolution?" "Yes, of course! That is why I resigned from my job. I am free now and ready to leave immediately!" His emotional response came right away: "I can't express my happiness and my pride enough! Your decision suits your way of thinking, something I have always valued in you." I laughed like a little boy and teased him: "How proud are you of me really?" "I'm very proud of you," he said, "in fact, I see my young self in you."

We looked at each other for a while. Then I looked at my mother. She looked tired and sad. She did not say a single word. She seemed utterly concerned about the exchange she had just witnessed between my grandfather and me, although she must have known all along that I would leave Colombia to fight in Palestine or in another faraway country without any hesitation.

My grandfather took care of my travel arrangements. He called a travel agency and booked a ticket for me to leave from Cartagena to Marseilles in France, thence to the Palestinian port of Haifa. He had carefully planned my itinerary. I was to leave Cartagena after ten days on board a French ship that would sail from New York via Cartagena to Marseilles.

The next day, I finished all my trip preparations first, and then visited the office of the secret Socialist Party, where

Antonio of Bethlehem

I met a number of my comrades. We talked about the political situation in Colombia and the increasing influence of American companies in South America. They were making incredible amounts of profit, because the owners were greedy businessmen who crushed countries under their feet, having suppressed people for hundreds of years. We discussed the American hegemony that overpowered South American countries by force, with military strength, through financial coups, spies and assassinations of those who refused its rules. Americans had plundered the natural resources of South America, subduing the people and installing mercenaries who took orders from Washington.

We also talked about the world-wide events, including the civil war in Spain. One of our comrades shared with us detailed information about that war and the role leftist organizations played in helping the Spanish republic stand against fascism, which confirmed that hundreds of South Americans fought in it.

Eventually, I told my comrades about the Palestinian revolt, how it was prompted by the various classes of people against the British authority and the Jewish emigration. I gave them the news about my upcoming departure to Palestine to join the said revolt.

Our comrade in charge responded: "You had better go to Spain to defend the republic that fights a violent war against fascism." I answered him with passion: "Let me explain my position. I chose to fight in Palestine because it is the land of my ancestors and because my decision is in line with the principles of our party: for the sake of freedom for all."

I was proud of my reply and saw respect on my comrades' faces. I had, after all, been listening intently to their opinions as far as our party's stance against colonialism and oppression. Then I bid farewell. They wished me success and a safe return to bring to them good news about the Palestinians' victory.

For an entire week before my trip, my family did not leave me alone one single moment. I was in the midst of my grandfather and my parents the entire time. They had so much to say to me. All along, they expressed such emotions that I had never witnessed before; my grandfather, in particular. His excitement dominated his words as he described Bethlehem and asked me to visit those parts of the city that he was especially fond of.

On the day of my trip, I was unable to control my emotions during my farewell to my family. Each of their words touched me deeply. We left for the airport together. It was raining heavily. All of us stayed under one umbrella.

I hugged my mother several times as she wept while repeating the same wish affectionately: "Please come back safe and sound." I walked very slowly towards the plane and waved to my family before going in.

Thanks to my beloved grandfather's careful planning, I was all set to continue with my journey on a French ship that would sail from New York via Cartagena to Marseilles.

Antonio of Bethlehem

Chapter Fourteen

Antonio of Bethlehem

Samih Masoud

It was time for me to get on the ship, called "Jeanne D'Arc". She left the port on time and started sailing on a clear weather, cruising near Panama and a few small islands on the Caribbean Sea, such as the French Antilles, St. Keats Islands and St. Lucia on the eastern side near the Atlantic Ocean.

Jeanne D'Arc was full of passengers of various nationalities. Soon, the waves began to pound her heavily. When night fell, she was crossing the Atlantic Ocean at full speed.

I shared a cabin with a man who spoke neither Spanish nor English. As I did not speak French, I tried to communicate with him in sign language. The cabin was comfortable, easy to relax in, which passengers needed because the trip to Marseilles was to take a month.

One evening, as I was sitting near the ship's front, I heard someone chanting in Arabic. I did not understand the lyrics because I did not speak Arabic. I approached the person. When he noticed that I was listening to him, he stopped singing and asked me in Spanish if I spoke Arabic. I told him that I did not, adding, "Although it's my grandfather's language!"

"Are you of Arabic origin?" he asked. "Yes!" I said, "I was born in Colombia but we're originally from Bethlehem, Palestine." He said excitedly. "I am from Chile but I'm also originally from Bethlehem. My name is Ibrahim Lama." I also gave him my name, and later, we started spending our time together. I came to know that he was a film director and that he and his brother, Badr Lama, had a movie company in Alexandria, Condor Film. Through their business, they were involved with writing, composing and production. In fact, in 1927, they produced the first Arabic film, "A Kiss in the Desert". Then they moved to Cairo where they produced many films that were considered the beginning of the Arabic cinema, both silent and sound.

Ibrahim's talks about the movie industry were very interesting. He gave me insights that I did not have before. I was enchanted with what he was telling me.

One evening, as we were walking on the deck under a clear, star-laden sky, with the waves hitting the ship, Ibrahim talked about romance in cinema. I asked him, "Why did you not build your company in Palestine?" He looked at me, smiling, and said: "When I left Chile with my brother, our destination was Haifa where we intended to start our movie business. However, we changed our plan when the ship stopped in Alexandria." He added: "We should have started our business in Haifa, because Haifa and all the Palestinian cities would have been worth our while."

We kept meeting during our long trip. We conversed on various subjects regarding Palestine. I told him about the revolution and my actual reason for going there: hoping that it would end victoriously.

In deep thought, he put his hand on his forehead and said: "I hope that the revolt is immune to the influence of the traditional Palestinian leadership so that it can avoid its many mistakes." He then added: "My examinations of the political situation in Palestine led me to one conclusion: the current leadership reveled in insignificant powers and demonstrated its increased tendencies toward autocracy, but also unquestionably played a role in the disputes and violent eruptions among feuding families and clans."

I forced myself to tender my response: "I do hope that the revolution's leaders work for the people." He looked at me and said: "I hope for the same!"

Samih Masoud

Days passed by slowly as the ship was sailing through the Atlantic Ocean. I was spending all my time chatting with Ibrahim. He spoke emotionally about Palestine, Egypt and Chile. I very much enjoyed our conversations. He gave me a lot of information on political, historical and social matters, and I shared with him my political views.

One day, as Ibrahim and I was conversing about his new film projects, I noticed land in the horizon. He saw my reaction and announced: "Yes, it's France!'

I was excited to see the blue of the ocean blending into the colors of the terrain. The buildings and tall trees created a striking scene, which stirred my imagination. Ibrahim's voice pulled me back to reality: "Do you know anyone in Marseilles?" "No, I know no one." He told me that he had a friend from Bethlehem, Nassif Eesa who lived in Marseilles and took him as his guest a few times.

Right at that moment, we heard the ship siren as she started moving into the port. The siren became louder, signaling the end of the trip.

After we disembarked, Ibrahim and I attended to the entry procedures for France. I was about to say goodbye to him, but he said, "Let's stay together until it's time for me to leave for Alexandria." He then asked me to accompany him to his friend's house who lived in the old city near Rue du Panier, the famous street for handcrafts.

We walked through several streets, before we arrived in the old city. His friend's house was big and beautiful. I thought it was a landmark on that street. We stood in front of it. Nassif came out right away and welcomed us warmly. Once inside, he insisted that we must stay with him as his guests as long as we needed. Ibrahim stayed for three days before his ship left for Alexandria, and I stayed for a week. I enjoyed listening to my host telling me about his life in Bethlehem before he had immigrated to France.

I respected Nassif very much for his support of the Palestinian resistance movement. He told me about his close connections with three fighters. One of them was living in Bethlehem, another in Jineen and the third, in Tulkarm. He promised to give me their addresses before I left Marseilles. I was utterly excited when he told me about them and their participation in the revolt. He reassured me that I could depend on his friends who would introduce me to the leaders of the revolution so that I might start my life as a fighter more effectively. Nassif was thus instrumental in my involvement with the Palestinian revolution.

Chapter Fifteen

Antonio of Bethlehem

Samih Masoud

Today is my last day in Marseilles. Early in the morning, Nassif and I sat in his dining room and had breakfast together. We talked mainly about the latest news on the Palestinian situation published in French newspapers. Full of enthusiasm, my host talked about a series of important developments. He mentioned the names of some of his friends who were active in the resistance movement. For a moment, I had the feeling that he was suppressing a deep desire. I was right in my instinct, as he said out loud: "I wish I were with them!"

"In a few days, I shall be with them. Your role as a successful business man who supports them is no less than what they are doing in the battle!" Pleased with my words on his importance, he reached to a pile of papers, took one out and explained, "These are the names and addresses of my three friends. Hide this list well!"

After Nassif handed over the list to me, he relaxed. I was to find his friends as soon as I arrived in Palestine. They would then inform me about the situation there and decide when I could join the resistance. My lack of Arabic language proficiency needed to be remedied.

Nassif accompanied me to the harbor. I was going to be on a ship, called "Normandi" which was scheduled to sail to Haifa. After finishing my travel arrangements, Nassif and I shook hands. I said to him affectionately: "It's time for a goodbye!"

Nassif waited in the harbor and we waved to one another until the ship left the port, and I kept looking at Marseilles until it disappeared from the horizon.

I walked a lot on the deck. The many passengers wearing Jewish skullcaps attracted my attention. I also noticed the presence of the Orthodox Jews, the Haredi with their long beards coming down to their chests and side curls. Out of curiosity, I asked one of the workers on the ship about them. He said that most of them were Polish, emigrating to Palestine which they call "The Promised Land". When I asked him if that claim was historically true, he answered nonchalantly, "It's power that makes it true!" I said to myself, yes, it's power and the imperialists who want the land of my ancestors.

One day, I stood near the bow. I was fascinated by the waves pounding the ship and then scattering back to the sea. When one of the Haredi came to stand near me, I thought of the grievous Jewish emigration to Palestine. Without any introduction, he asked me why I never prayed when eating at the ship restaurant. He then remarked, "You also do not participate in group prayers in the prayer hall." I asked him: "Does a Christian have to pray your way?"

"He has no right to pray with us!" was his response. After that outburst, he sat beside me and bombarded me with many questions. I told him that I was a tourist from Colombia and wanted to visit the holy places in Palestine. I talked about the Christian pilgrimage rituals. I was astonished to find out that he was well aware of them. I said to him, "Your insights will help me when I perform the required rituals." Looking at me with examining eyes, he uttered a request, "Tell me about your country, Colombia."

I gave him detailed information: that it was a large country in South America on both the Atlantic and the Pacific oceans – with large areas on the Caribbean Sea; The Andes; The Amazon River – world's largest and second longest river that springs out of The Andes; the production of about 60% of the world emeralds; a thousand kinds of plants, animals and birds and our Cano Crystal River – the most beautiful river in the world with its natural mix of mesmerizing colors during different seasons.

Listening to me carefully, he commented, "It sounds like your country is beautiful. It must be an excellent place for tourists. Is it not?"

"Yes, Colombia is a rare natural masterpiece. You can think of it as one of the most attractive countries for sightseeing."

I ran into him one other day when he asked me more about Colombia. Once again, I gave him many details. I also had a question for him: "Why is it that you don't want to settle down in Colombia instead of Palestine?"

"Your question surprises me. In its first conference in Basel, Switzerland in 1897, the Zionist Movement had focused on two alternatives as far as the best place for a Jewish state: Argentine and Palestine. Eventually, Palestine was preferred for religious reasons. God had promised his prophet Jacob to give him Palestine."

I didn't hold anything back when I talked to him about the grim conditions under which Palestinian Arabs suffer because of the British imperialist rule that supports Jews against Arabs, in line with the Zionist incentive.

He kept quiet for a moment. Then he showed his eagerness to go to the "Promised Land". He expressed his passionate love for Jerusalem with hand movements as if he was drawing the city's old quarters – drawing them from misconceptions. I felt sad hearing him talk about Palestine in this way. I felt is if he was stabbing me in the heart, because he was voicing the Zionist thoughts and the British imperialist agenda. Their shared interest was to occupy my homeland, uproot my people and install a Zionist state over what they falsely claim to be the promised land of Jews.

Antonio of Bethlehem

On a sunny morning, I was standing near the bow again. As I was scanning the sea, I noticed a land far away. My excitement and happiness grew as the ship moved closer. My trip was about to end.

The passengers gathered on the deck. Normandi was moving fast towards Haifa. I felt as if I was flying over magnificent Mount Carmel (Mount Mar Elias). The captain was blowing the siren as a welcome to the military boats that came to accompany the ship. The British flag was soaring on those boats. I shall always remember that sad sight, for it was a physical proof of the British support for the Jewish settlers in Palestine as well as the power of the Zionist Movement.

Eventually, Normandi anchored at the designated wharf and the passengers began to leave. There was a great number of people receiving the new Jewish settlers, beaming all over with joy.

I had to wait in a long line. When I reached the British officer in charge, he requested my immigration papers. "I'm a Colombian citizen and I want to perform my Christian pilgrimage rituals." He looked surprised and asked me loudly: "How can you do that in these difficult circumstances?" I responded with a question: "Are the Christian holy places in danger?" He said, "No", looked through my passport and then stamped it.

I left the port quickly and found myself in the old part of Haifa. I was about to start my life anew in the land of my ancestors.

Chapter

Sixteen

Antonio of Bethlehem

Samih Masoud

I arrived in Haifa on the last day of June 1936. From the first moment on, I was enchanted by its beauty. It felt strange to have to look at Mount Carmel from a distance.

Roaming through Haifa, I was overcome with utter joy. The houses, built with smooth white stones were especially beautiful. I looked all around and ended up in its many different parts, from the sea shore up to the top of Mount Carmel.

The promise I had made to my grandfather stayed with me all the time: to visit all the cities and villages of Palestine. Here I was in Haifa, touching its soil. How happy I felt familiarizing myself with Haifa, whose image was going to remain in my memory for the rest of my life! I started my exploration of the city in the Al Hanateer (cabriolets) Square. The driver took me to the German Quarter. He drove on the main street, a straight line from the shore. He then drove higher towards the rocky slopes of Mount Carmel. Its tall trees and green plants were in clear sight now.

Later on, I continued to go through Haifa on foot, carrying my suitcase. I did not know where to go to spend the night. Then I spotted an inn at the German Quarter. I went in and booked a room for three nights. The innkeeper welcomed me warmly when he saw my passport. He told me that he had some relatives in Aroca who had migrated to Colombia long time ago.

I spoke in English with him about Haifa and Colombia. He welcomed me even more enthusiastically, when I told him that my roots go back to Bethlehem. He introduced himself to me by the name of Abu Ali. The pain in his voice while he talked about the political situation in Palestine touched me deeply. When he invited me to dinner in his house nearby, I was caught by surprise. I accepted his gracious invitation wholeheartedly. He told me that he would be expecting me at seven.

Since the dinner hour was still a bit away, I went to my room on the third floor and sat on the balcony. I very much enjoyed the view of Haifa with its nearby sceneries. When it was almost seven, I walked down to the reception area where I saw Abu Ali who welcomed me, "You are like me, right on time!" We left the inn right away. I was enchanted with his house. A garden full of beautiful flowers greeted us. We went inside and sat in a large room. He told me about his home and some of the well-known houses in Haifa. He particularly stressed those of the Khoury and Khayyat families and that of Shaikh Abd al-Rahman Murad. We then went into the dining room. We kept talking over a meal of kabab (grilled meat) about Palestine.

Abu Ali primarily focused on the Jewish Agency, the Jewish mobilization and the transfer of Ottoman lands to the Jews under the British Mandate. He reached to the conclusion that the armed revolt came about as a reaction to the Zionist actions and the British Authority.

I enjoyed our conversation on the matters that troubled me as well and felt the need to let him know about my intent to join the Palestinian Revolution. His view was that the revolt was taking the right path in spite of some bad mistakes The Arab Higher Committee had committed. I asked him about that leadership. He was ready to share with me what he knew: "You should be aware of the unwritten Palestinian agenda, especially since you have traveled all this way to contribute to it with little information about your ancestors' homeland."

Samih Masoud

Thanks to Abu Ali, I now knew that The Arab Higher Committee was the political body which represented the Palestinians under the British Mandate. It was founded in 1936 after a civil rebellion and comprised right-wing parties that were formed by prominent families.

Abu Ali gave me details about the leader of the said committee, explaining that even his closest comrades confirm that his policy was extemporaneous and that he was quite the dictator, especially when it came to military matters. I asked, "What are the sources of this information?" "It was all in a memorandum of a vital dignitary from Haifa who was a right-hand man to the committee leader. That dignitary had written his missive as his conscience dictated it." I thanked my host for the valuable insights he had shared with me. He responded humbly: "I only want you to learn the facts."

"How can I meet Khaled al-Jilani, one of the men in charge of the revolt in Jineen?" I asked Abu Ali. I quickly explained to him that he happens to be a friend of a businessman in Marseilles whom I met for the first time there where I had to wait for my transportation to Haifa."

Abu Ali knew of Khaled al-Jilani: "He is one of the most critical members of the Palestinian resistance movement. I shall introduce you to a man who can take you to him." I thanked him enthusiastically for his help and for his brotherly welcome.

Antonio of Bethlehem

Chapter Seventeen

Antonio of Bethlehem

During the next three days, I discovered more about the charming Haifa. On the fourth day, I met Saleh, the man who would accompany me to my next destination. I bid farewell to Abu Ali and went with Saleh to the bus station. We took a bus to Jineen. We left from the Al Hanateer Square, going first through the al-Nassera Street, then moving on to a big road through several enchanting villages. Saleh knew how to speak English: "Our country is beautiful. It is like a paradise." He then spurted out: "You must learn Arabic! It is an important part of your identity." I agreed enthusiastically and repeated to him my desire to become proficient in my ancestors' tongue.

My travel companion continued to talk about the importance of the Arabic language and its relationship to the Arabic culture. I was happy to acquire a wealth of information from him.

I was curious about his interests outside that which we had been talking about: "Do you have any connection to the world of writing and literature?" His answer came as a pleasant surprise to me: "I am a union member and always try to include some literary texts in my speeches, especially lines from our national poetry."

The subject then was moved to the Palestinian freedom movement. He gave me insights into the organization of the union. He cited many names, going back to 1923 when the first nucleus of the league came to life.

I was particularly intrigued by Saleh's story of a young Palestinian by the name of Michel Mitri who came from Argentina and founded a liberation union with his extensive knowledge and experience in such organizations. I had assumed to be the first one to come from South America to Palestine. Yet now, I was hearing the name of another man who was here before me and was going to live on in the collective memory of Palestinians. He dominated my thoughts and inspired me to put all my strength toward my own potential.

I told Saleh how I felt. I wanted to waste no time to begin doing what I had come here for. Michel's story paralleled my grandfather's hopes for me. I decided never to leave this path because Palestine was worth everything to me, as my roots were in its soil. Saleh confirmed that Palestine was worth everything to us all.

We continued our conversation about our homeland until the bus arrived in Jineen. We stopped near the municipality building. After exiting the bus, we walked to the house of one of his friends. That friend opened the door with a hearty welcome: "My house is yours!" We introduced ourselves to one another. This dear man, Ahmad, told me that he had a friend from Bait Jala whose name was Anton.

Saleh and Ahmad left later on, asking me to wait for them in the house. They were out for a while. When they came back, Khaled al-Jilani was with them. He hugged me and asked me in proper English, "How is my friend Nassif?"

"He's fine." I said. I told him a lot about Nassif and his business in Marseilles and about his passionate interest in the Palestinian revolution. Khaled looked happy upon hearing what I said, and commented tenderly: "He's my comrade for life!"

He then looked at his watch and said calmly, "It is midnight now, and I shall put you on a difficult test as we go on foot to a place outside Jineen. I will introduce you to the field commander there." I said goodbye to Saleh and Ahmad. Khaled and I went to the main street and left Jineen westward through a rugged road, surrounded by figs and olive trees. We then took another road in a valley.

I saw a village at a distance over a high plateau. As we got closer, I noticed that some houses and arches were built in the style of Arabic architecture. I thought we reached our destination. However, we continued to walk on a road paved with small pebbles. "We're almost there." Khaled announced in a low voice.

We walked up to the top of a mountain. Fatigued, we arrived in a place where we met three men who were heavily armed. They asked Khaled for the password, which he uttered immediately. We were thus allowed to accompany them to a large cave, with many guards standing at its entrance.

When we went in, we found a group of men waiting for us. In the middle was a tall and robust man wearing the traditional Arabic head cover (kufiyya & iqal). Khaled introduced me to him and to his comrades, while he told me that man was one of the chief leaders of the revolt – without mentioning his name. Khaled was talking in Arabic, but I sensed that he was talking about me.

Everyone listened to Khaled with utmost attention. Then the leader began to talk. In a loud voice, he thanked me for the stand I take regarding the revolution. He was talking in Arabic, and Khaled was translating everything into English for me. The leader had mentioned much information about the Palestinian national liberation movement, but he had also emphatically pointed out the obstacle I had: I did not know Arabic. His suggestion for me was to join the police force that the civil administration of the British Mandate had formed so that I could provide the revolution with essential services.

Antonio of Bethlehem

I asked softly: "How can I join the police?" The answer came from the leader. "Don't you worry. Khaled will give you the necessary help." I was utterly moved by the leader's confidence in me and accepted his advice immediately. That comforting exchange was followed by many stories the other men told, and Khaled filled me in with his translations yet once again. After a while, Khaled and I left the cave. The leader wished me a successful application to the British Mandate's police department.

Khaled and I walked back to Jineen on the same rugged road. Then Khaled arranged a secure place for me to live. The next day, together with some of his comrades, he took care of all the necessary procedures for me to join the said police force. Thanks to their efforts, I acquired a position at the Tarsala Center near the village of Jaba'.

Winning the confidence of the British officers was crucial. So, I was eager to get close to them. Whatever information I obtained from those officers, I passed on to Khaled. The leadership analyzed everything and planned military initiatives to take the British forces by surprise in battles. Skirmishes to be prompted by the Palestinian national liberation groups were planned to take place in different parts of Palestine. What was referred to as the "Mountain of Fire" had a special importance as the primary focus of the movement's leadership.

I was always thrilled to hear from Khaled that I was providing the movement with an excellent intelligence service and that the leaders appreciated my efforts greatly.

Chapter Eighteen

Antonio of Bethlehem

Samih Masoud

After some time at the Tarsala Center, I decided to visit Bethlehem. The police chief gave me a one week-vacation to perform my Christian pilgrimage rituals. I left for the holy city in a car that belonged to the British Mandate police force. The driver, an Arab, gave me some details about the many villages and cities we passed by, such as Nablus, Tulkarm, Ramallah, Bait Sahoor and Bait Jala.

I was extremely happy when we arrived in Bethlehem. The driver let me out near the Church of the Nativity. I saw some narrow alleys near the church. I looked joyfully at some old houses built with white stones.

I entered the Church of the Nativity where Jesus Christ was born and is considered one of the oldest churches not only in Palestine but in the world. I roamed through all parts of the church and the cavern located on the lower side. I descended there through a narrow ladder. I noticed the silver star at the manger that was decorated with alabaster. It had a writing in Latin: "Here, Jesus Christ was born from Virgin Mary." I also noticed the fifteen lamps that decorated the nativity grotto, representing Christian denominations.

I left the Church of the Nativity and stopped in front of a few nearby churches and monasteries of different Christian groups. Then I passed by charming alleys that transported me in time, as if I was seeing that holy city through my grandfather's eyes.

I went into the first hotel I saw in one of the alleys. When the owner learned that my family roots were in Bethlehem, he gave me a special room. He was in his eighties. Hoping that he might recognize some names, I showed him a list of my grandfather's relatives and friends. He looked at the names carefully and said that all those people had died. I also showed him the name of Nassif's

Antonio of Bethlehem

friend. "Yes, I know him well! He is a relative of mine, a member of the Hananiyya family. He migrated to Chile with his family last year, but I don't know anything beyond that."

Since the hotel owner did not know any one of my grandfather's relatives or friends, I decided not to stay in Bethlehem and to go to Jerusalem instead.

The next morning, I went to the city center where I hailed a cab, asking the driver to take me to Jerusalem. I was filled with excitement to see that holy city. Eventually, the city plateau and its Mount of Olives began to emerge in the horizon.

The taxi stopped near the Damascus Gate. I got out and booked a room in one of the hotels nearby. Then I went to the old city. I walked inside the city wall in narrow and winding alleys and streets that were filled with people. I was enchanted by the old houses with their arched doors and windows, near which stood columns of marble with beautifully engraved crowns.

I walked on Via Dolorosa (The Road of Pains) that passes through old Jerusalem's alleys – the path on which Jesus Christ had walked, carrying his cross from the al-Asbat Gate to the Church of the Holy Sepulcher. That church was built on the rock, over which Jesus Christ was crucified. The Church of the Holy Sepulcher is considered the holiest and most important Christian church on Earth, because it holds the Holy Tomb where Jesus Christ was buried and from where his body rose to Heaven. I spent some time by this tomb. It is cube-shaped, surrounded by polished marble columns in the middle of the church, with a large dome over its many columns.

I stood for a while in the churchyard. It is large and paved with many small pebbles. On the right, there are parallel lines of steps on which visitors sit after having visited the church, enjoying the sight of the church architecture with its many arches and vaults.

Afterward, I visited the Omar ibn al-Khattab Mosque that was adjacent to the Church of the Holy Sepulcher. Then I visited the Holy Dome and the al-Aqsa Mosque. I was seeing its high minarets for the first time in my life. I loved the characteristic shapes of arches and colonnades with old vaults, supported by columns with crowns covered with beautifully colored engravings.

I woke up early on my second day in Jerusalem. When I went to the dining room downstairs to have breakfast, I noticed the headlines on a newspaper, the English print of *The Palestine Post*: Galilee's British governor Andrews and his assistant were assassinated by Arab revolutionaries. I immediately left for the hotel reception and checked out. I then went to the nearest police station where I presented my papers to the person in charge and asked him to help me return to my post at the Tarsala Center.

Luckily, a truck was about to leave for Jineen and I was able to arrive at my post in the afternoon. I noticed the tension at the center. I heard the plans to strike the Palestinian national liberation movement in order to exterminate it as a response to the assassination of a man in such a high position. As time passed, these plans became clearer. I collected whatever details I could and passed them immediately on to Khaled.

Events were never-ending. The British forces had become more militant toward the revolutionaries. In its ensuing stages, the Palestinian resistance movement was going to have to face a much stronger resistance. The committee in charge of the investigation of the assassination had advised a division of the country between Arabs and Zionists. These new initiatives, however, were short-lived, as the resistance movement was able to regain its momentum. In the summer of 1938, it had reached its highpoint as large areas in the north and in central Palestine were under its control.

The revolutionaries were able to take over many cities, demonstrating their organizational skills as well as their efficiency in guerilla warfare. They were punishing land brokers, spies and mercenaries. The revolt leaders became the actual rulers of numerous territories.

This development persisted for a good while, but then the resistance fighters started to retreat as internal fighting between armed comrades took place. Political assassinations had turned into a movement of eradication that hit both the good and the bad. Traitors and British mercenaries spread everywhere, which severely altered the revolt's fate.

Amid all the violent turmoil, the chief revolt commander Abu-Kamal who, together with his armed comrades and with great courage, had waged a battle against the British enemy, fell as a martyr. When I saw the pictures of Abu-Kamal in Palestinian newspapers, I was shocked to note that he was the same man whom I had met in the cave – the one who had suggested that I get involved in the intelligence service to support the revolt's timely undertakings. I grieved his martyrdom. He was still at the peak of his life and combat abilities. I told my feelings to Khaled but also stressed emphatically the fact that revolutionaries never die, for history will always remembered them.

After Abu-Kamal's martyrdom, the revolutionary forces retreated. Another factor in that outcome was the interference of some Arabic countries which wanted the revolution to be stopped after Britain retracted its decision to divide Palestine, but especially in view of the likelihood of a second world war. Thus, the Palestinian resistance movement ceased to exist, and the British army was able to control the entire country.

Antonio of Bethlehem

Chapter

Nineteen

Antonio of Bethlehem

Samih Masoud

Three months after the end of the revolution in 1939, for which I had come to Palestine, I decided to return to Colombia. I resigned my official post at the Tarsala Center. After a farewell, I spent a few days with Khaled al-Jilani. We reminisced about the virtues of Abu-Kamal as a rare Palestinian revolt leader.

Before my departure, I said to Khaled in Arabic, which I had already mastered, that his name would permanently mark many stories on the resistance movement. I added that I will always remember him inside my mental images of Palestinian villages and cities with their valleys, plateaus and mountains. His brotherly words in response touched me deeply. I could barely hold back my tears.

I left for Haifa from where I boarded a French ship to Marseilles. Two weeks later, I arrived there. I went to Nassif's house. I shared with him my experiences in Palestine. He cried hard when I told him the reason for the revolution's end after having marked its presence as an important part of the Palestinian history.

I stayed with Nassif for a few days. I then continued my trip to Cartagena. This time, I was on an American ship. About one month later, I arrived in Cartagena. From there, I went to Bogotá.

I arrived at home on a summer day. I was hugged heartily by my family. I asked where my grandfather was.

In heavy sobs, they told me that my beloved grandfather had passed away. He had fallen ill shortly before his death. He was so eager to know about how I was doing in Palestine. Sorrow filled me. Each of the moments I had spent with him came alive, especially his talks with me about his memories of Bethlehem, but Palestine in general. The names of his many old relatives and friends were still in my mind.

I asked my father to take me to my grandfather's grave. My entire family accompanied me. Everybody was silent. I sat by his grave where I placed a wreath of roses. Per my wish, my family left me there alone for a while.

The next day, I visited my party's headquarters where my comrades welcomed me back warmly. They wanted to hear all about my experiences inside the Palestinian resistance movement during the past three years. I told them in detail about all that I had lived. They took great interest in what I had to say and asked me many questions. Their intense attention to my answers was an evidence for me that they were ready to fight for freedom everywhere – may that be in Colombia, Palestine, in other South American countries or anywhere else.

About a month later, our party held its annual meeting and I was elected to serve as a member of the central committee. In order for me to devote all my time to my party's undertakings, it was decided that I should work fulltime in the office to supervise all organizational matters.

My new position gave me the responsibility to familiarize myself with all the leftist parties in South America. It also enabled me to participate in their conferences and activities, establish connections with all the members and learn more about their progressive thoughts and initiatives to help eliminate the current problems.

Samih Masoud

While I was excited about my intensified involvement with my party's objectives, my passion for the Palestinian cause did not lessen. I kept up with the recent political developments in Palestine, either through international journalistic articles or with the help of Khaled's letters. After the end of World War II, I was dismayed to discover the American interference, which had become the most instrumental source of advantage for the Zionists. The US influence was especially evident in the intensified Jewish emigration after Britain had left its command over the Palestinian land. The agenda was about establishing a Jewish state in Palestine.

I was utterly worried. The national Palestinian movement was facing a grave danger. The decisive battle with the Zionists was certainly on its way, and I had to be in it. I felt a strong urge in spite of my knowledge that the enemy was stronger, better organized and better prepared.

I decided to go to go back to Palestine. My party's central committee granted me the necessary permission. One morning at the beginning of the year 1946, I said farewell to my family and flew to Paris on board a Colombian airplane. After three days of waiting in Paris, I took a plane to Beirut. From there, I went onto another flight; this time, to Lydda. I stayed a few days in that small city. I met with Khaled there, per the telegram he had sent to me to Bogotá.

We drove to Jerusalem. On the way, we talked passionately on many matters concerning Palestine, including the scarcity of arms and the weakness of the military and organizational efforts. We both knew the reason: the British Mandate had been against the armament of the Arabs. Its policies opened only for Jews the doors to arms and equipment supplies.

Antonio of Bethlehem

Khaled told me that he had joined the Holy Jihad Army whose general commander was trying to revive the Palestinian national liberation movement. My immediate response was: "I also would like to join its military forces." Smiling, he embraced my eagerness: "You were successful in the intelligence service. The Holy Jihad Army could use your skills, but in a capacity other than that of an ordinary fighter." I agreed: "In that case, we must find an effective role for me." He said: "Let's think about this matter together!"

We had reached Jerusalem. We checked in to a hotel near the Hebron Gate on the western wall of the old city.

Chapter Twenty

Antonio of Bethlehem

Samih Masoud

The next day, I woke up early in the morning and went to a popular restaurant on al-Wad Street. I ordered the traditional breakfast that was popular in Jerusalem. It consisted of toasted round bread mixed with sesame seeds, falafel and eggs. I then left for Khan al-Zait Street. On my way, I bought a copy of the English issue of *The Palestine Post* and went into a well-liked café.

I leafed through the paper, reading the local and international news. I learned about the increasing influence of the United States in the Middle East. Through its transcontinental oil companies and its loyalty to the British policies regarding the empowerment of the Zionist Lobby, the U.S. had now replaced the United Kingdom's rule – once again to the disadvantage of Palestinians.

I noticed a job announcement from the American consulate for a driver who knew the city well. I got excited about this opportunity. I left the café right away and rushed to the American consulate. The man at the reception desk asked me a few questions upon hearing my interest for the advertised driver-position. Once he saw in my papers that I was from Colombia and heard that I spoke English very well, he gave me a form to fill and told me to check for a response in a week.

When I saw Khaled that evening, I told him about my application to the American consulate. He was very happy about this news: "This is an important post. If you get it, you'll be close to the important decision makers." "It was good that I noticed the job announcement. If I become a driver, I can do some intelligence work in favor of our national cause." Khaled's eyes were lit up when he said: "I do hope that you'll get that position!"

Antonio of Bethlehem

In the following days, I was busy meeting my new comrades in the Holy Jihad Army. Khaled introduced me to some resistance fighters with distinguished attributes. I was especially moved listening to three men: Fadhel Rasheed, an Iraqi officer who had left behind a delightful life and came to Jerusalem to fight for Palestine. On account of his remarkable background, he was able to attain a high position in the military. Fawzi al-Qutub had great field skills. Yusuf al-Rashmawi also had made his mark as an excellent combatant.

A week later, I went back to the consulate where the man in charge received me with a smile: "Based on the information in your application, we found you to be the best among the candidates. Congratulations on your driver-position for the general consul!"

I thanked him and went through all the required procedures. I hid my emotions when he warned me against Arabs: "He who befriends them will be fired." He then gave me a pass which was going to allow me entrance to the consulate during work hours. I was to start the job next morning.

After I left the consulate, I first went to my hotel, and from there, to Khaled. I gave him the good news. He didn't hide his excitement, "It's a critical starting point! Through your position, you'll accomplish a lot of things for Palestine."

The next morning, I went to the consulate. The receptionist instructed me to always stay in the drivers' room, the one on the right on the first floor, that I was to receive my daily assignments there. I did as instructed. A short while later, I was informed about the places the consul wished to visit that day. Then I met the consul who sat in the back seat. He requested that I take him to the King David Hotel. I was surprised to hear him talk to me in fluent Spanish. He told me that he did not want to get out of the car; he only wanted to see the extent of the explosion that had taken place a few days ago as a reaction against the British Mandate in Palestine. The said hotel was the target of the attack. In a low voice, he said: "Begin has done it!"

The hotel was indeed exploded by the orders of Menachem Begin, head of the Irgun Zionist Organization. His demand was carried out by the members in his organization who were disguised as Arabs. The attack was described as one of the most notorious terrorist acts in Palestine.

Later on, I drove the consul to the office of the British High Commissioner. I waited for him for three hours before taking him back to the consulate. With time, I realized that the consul most frequently – almost on a daily basis – visited the Zionist organizations, specifically the Jewish Agency.

Due to these repeated visits, my face was now known among the Jewish Agency guards. I learned their names and work hours. I spoke with them for extended periods of times, especially on those occasions when I came alone to take care of some consulate business. I thus won their trust. They began to let the consul's car in without a search.

They seemed happy that the developments in Palestine were in their favor. They spoke with great enthusiasm about their forthcoming state in Palestine. Whenever I asked them about that subject, they answered in the same way. These conversations were suffocating me. But

Antonio of Bethlehem

any information I was able to get from them was critical, as I was gathering valuable data for my commander on the other side of Jerusalem.

Chapter
Twenty-One

Antonio of Bethlehem

Samih Masoud

One day in February 1947, I had a conversation with some of my comrades in the Holy Jihad Army. We discussed the decision the British government had taken to leave Palestine and to bring the conflict to the attention of the United Nations. Once again, we discussed the fact that Britain's initiative was geared toward the formation of a Jewish state in Palestine. The Jews had already established a strong, well-trained military force in the area. It would be not at all difficult for them to fulfill their ambitious plans.

Days passed by after Britain abandoned the mandate. The signs of war could be seen everywhere. The stark contrast between the Zionists' sophisticated supplies and superior military forces and the meager means in the hands of the Palestinians always prompted a deep sadness in me. I often fell into despair because of the incomparable differences. Nor was a careful look at the defense capacity of other Arabic countries was any help to my desperation. The Zionists were backed by the powerful British after all.

In such times of anguish, my thoughts would shift between reality and an imagined reality. I would conceive of possible ways to defend Palestine purely through my passionate love and die as a martyr defending my ancestors' homeland.

With time, I became obsessed with the possibility of blowing up the Zionist Organizations Assembly. I examined all the steps of my plan and the potential of its success. I knew I had to depend on my personal interactions with the Jewish Agency guards. I thought of loading the American consulate car with a large number of explosives and entering the compound without being searched. I would then blow up the front of the building. That organization had, after all,

Antonio of Bethlehem

played a major role in encouraging Jewish immigration into Palestine and the settlement of Jews there.

I laid out my plan to a small committee of commanders of the Holy Jihad Army. After detailed discussions, there was agreement. Three commanders were going to provide the explosives.

One day in March 1948, I took the consulate car to Wadi al-Jawz where I entered the garage of a residential building. I was calm when I met with three comrades who were going to help me. In a short period of time, the explosives were loaded in that car's trunk. I went back to west Jerusalem and arrived at the Jewish Agency. I stopped in front of three guards and conversed with them for a little while about two guests I had come to take to the consulate.

They let me go in without a search. I parked the car in front of the main building. Leaving the car there, I rushed to the guarded gate, claiming that I had to buy some journals for the consulate. Within a few minutes, I reached the alleys of old Jerusalem. As I hid inside one of the houses, a big explosion shook the whole city.

I had to stay in hiding for several days. Then I met with Khaled in a location we had designated in advance. We went to a camp run by the Holy Jihad Army near the village of Abu-Dees. The chief commander welcomed me: "What you have done was very important to raise our morale." His Iraqi assistant remarked as zealously: "What you have accomplished was a most important operation against the Zionists."

Samih Masoud

I kept perusing my comrades' faces while they were thanking me. They were all in agreement that this operation, a historical milestone for Palestinians, would always be remembered by the present-day generations as well as by those to come. While they were all talking about the attack, one of the comrades started reading from *The Jewish Palestine Post*. An extensive report stated that the architect of this operation was highly skillful in hiding his Arabic origin under his Colombian citizenship; that the examination of his papers at the American Consulate had not revealed his connections to Palestine nor to the Palestinian national liberation movement.

All my comrades were utterly pleased with what they had just heard about me and the operation. The newspaper also reported that fatalities and serious injuries were high in number and that the building was severely damaged. As for political analysts, they were quoted as having evaluated this attack as one not to be forgotten.

Reading on from the same newspaper, our chief commander then announced: "Unfortunately, the Zionist leaders were in Tel Aviv at the time of the explosion; hence, they remain unharmed. Had they been in their offices during the attack, they would have been killed and their dream of a Jewish state would have been a thing of the past."

Antonio of Bethlehem

Chapter

Twenty-Two

Antonio of Bethlehem

Samih Masoud

I eliminated all the traces through which the American consulate could link me to Palestine before the operation. Here I was, having formally joined the forces of the Holy Jihad Army in an old barrack in Jerusalem, getting ready to engage in battles in defense of Jerusalem and all of Palestine.

In this new stage of my life, I felt livelier, having a greater ability to attack my enemies. There was a great change in me. Everything inside me woke up at once and pushed me to the road of armed resistance through the end. I knew, I could do nothing else but be involved actively in the Palestinian cause in spite of all the anticipated adversities that could lead to death.

Clashes in the March of 1948 became more intense than ever before. They included villages around Jerusalem and its southern and western entries, including the Lutron area, Bab al-Wad and Jerusalem / Bethlehem / al-Khalil roads. The Holy Jihad Army had taken extensive military actions and achieved victories in many battles which I fought together with my armed comrades, including the battle of al-Duhaysha near Bethlehem. I shall never forget the hero from Sahoor, Yusuf al-Rashmawi. He had exploded himself right in front of a Jewish tank he had stopped, killing whoever was inside.

The leaders of the Holy Jihad Army had been determined to be victorious, and they indeed had been. They took possession of many military equipment supplies as well as tanks, buses, trucks, guns and machineguns.

I also participated in the al-Misrara battle. Jewish forces had attacked that area, causing a great destruction in the buildings. Bombardments included that of Bab al-Amoud. The village of al-Qastal on the south end of the road to Jerusalem / Jaffa had also fallen. Due to its strategic location, it was controlling the supplies coming from Tel Aviv to the Jewish quarters in Jerusalem.

The chief commander of the Holy Jihad Army was in Damascus when al-Qastal fell. From the military agency of the League of Arab States, he requested arms. Despite his persistent pleas, he unfortunately did not receive the necessary ammunition. So, he had to return to Jerusalem with no support from the Arab states. On April 7, 1948, he went to al-Qastal to liberate the village with whatever he had available for his men. He was engaged in a battle for which the Jews were prepared incomparably better, as they were higher in number and combat supplies. The driving force behind our chief commander's fight in that battle, which left him face to face with death, was his commitment to the Palestinian national liberation cause. He was able to break the Jewish lines, but eventually, he fell as a martyr. He thus wrote a most glorious narrative on an epic heroism with his own blood.

I was near him when he fell as a martyr. Later on, I kept living through those moments. I was traumatized by his death. I suffered from a series of psychological disturbances.

About a month after the al-Qastal battle, the British left Palestine and the Jewish Agency immediately declared the birth of the Jewish state. Two great powers at that time, the Soviet Union and the United States of America recognized it at once. On the same day, the official Arab armed forces entered Palestine; but unfortunately, they were far weaker than the Jewish armed forces – whether in the number of their fighters or their equipment supplies. I was in grave despair at the sight of their weakness and their inability to confront the enemy.

Samih Masoud

The Arab armed forces engaged in several military operations, none of which had any impact on the imbalance that I have previously described. Thus, the war ended in favor of the Jewish army. The Jews occupied a large number of Palestinian villages and cities and uprooted countless Palestinians. The best known among the atrocities the Jewish armed forces committed is that of Dair Yaseen. As a result of the carnage there, thousands of Palestinians fled to nearby Arabic countries where they were lodged in special camps.

I was mortified with what was taking place in the land of my ancestors. It became clear to me that the Arabic governments merely witnessed what was happening. They did no more than wage an emotional word of the war in their radio stations. In my view, they were covering their failure to defend Palestine and its people. Their inaction resulted in an obvious emphasis on their trivial role in Palestine.

I was extremely worried about the devastating conditions of Palestinians. I had a hard time accepting the bitter defeat and the horrible tragedy of my people. I could see in my mind's eyes how they were forced to leave their homes and homeland. What always belonged to them and that for which they had worked all their lives were being handed over to the Jews.

A few days after a truce was signed between the Jewish state and the nearby Arabic countries, I was sure that war had come to an end. Therefore, I decided to go back to Colombia. I bid my Palestinian comrades farewell, reassuring them that I shall never forget them. They all responded with heartwarming words. The emotional utterances of Fadhel Rasheed and Khaled al-Jilani were especially moving.

Antonio of Bethlehem

Since I was being pursued by both the Jews and the British on account of the Jewish Agency attack in Jerusalem, my comrades prepared my documents with a pseudonym. They advised me to return to Colombia via Alexandria, not Haifa or Jaffa. It was particularly difficult to travel through Beirut because the Galilee area on the Lebanese border was occupied by the Jews.

I first went to Gaza where I stayed for a few days, and then took a cab to Rafah on the Egyptian border. From there, I took another cab to al-Areesh and entered Egypt with my altered papers.

I had to take a long desert road to Cairo, from where I went to Alexandria. It was a touristic city full of people from many countries. I stayed there for a few days, but did not move about as I was severely depressed because of the loss of Palestine. All I did there was buy a ticket to Colombia on an Italian ship.

Impatiently, I waited for the time the ship would leave Alexandria. I wanted to isolate myself in a cabin where I would sleep for a long time behind a locked door and forget my inability to fulfill my dream of a free Palestine.

Chapter Twenty-Three

Antonio of Bethlehem

Samih Masoud

I arrived in Bogotá with grief consuming me. My family was surprised to find me in such a poor psychological state. I thought of my grandfather and wondered what he would feel, had he been alive. His memory opened more wounds in me and made them bleed continuously. In actuality, he was still very much alive in my conscience and for my family.

On the next day after my arrival, I visited my party center. My comrades received me with a warm welcome, offering me many hugs. They avoided any talk about the Palestinian situation. The latest news was available to everyone through the local and foreign media anyway. They did, however, ask me about my experiences in Palestine, whether it was overall good or bad. They listened to me with great interest and gave me much encouragement, prompting in me a renewed hope.

After a few days, the party held a ceremony in honor of my return. Some leading members of the progressive parties were invited. The party's general secretary described me as an international fighter. I was pleased to hear him narrate some of my efforts in Palestine. He claimed that I was able to turn the dream of my ancestors into a reality with my initiatives in the Palestinian national liberation movement, which had an enduring effect on my life.

I returned to my position in the party as a member of the central committee. Soon, my comrades began to single me out as a key person for our cause. Their interest in my thoughts about the problems regarding politics at large grew. This interest was intensified after I published a number of articles about my experiences in Palestine and about the socialist ideology and its superior goals. The party's objective was to achieve justice for the people whom capitalist societies were oppressing while exploiting their existence as human beings.

I concluded my articles with one about the negative impact the U.S. companies had on South American countries. In that writing, I provided many examples of how those companies exploit a country's natural wealth; how their interferences exceed beyond the economic equation to include a strong political presence and engaging in military coups in order to install mercenary systems that work against the interests of the people.

Writing those articles gave me some relief as far as the trauma I suffered after the Palestinian defeat and invigorated me on an intellectual level. I was able to thus express in blunt honesty my antagonistic feelings toward the United States because of its support of the crimes committed by the Zionist movement in Palestine. Neither its economic, political and military interference in South American affairs, nor its forced policies that served the interests of the American capital against the development and prosperity of South American peoples escaped my analyses.

I shared my writings in many conferences in Colombia and some neighboring countries. Through my personal attendance in those conferences, I learned that South American countries were not only suffering under poverty and unemployment, but also were subjected to violence and narcotics trades under despotic regimes.

The conferences I attended gave me the opportunity to meet many people whose thinking process was in sync with mine. I embraced them with great pleasure as they expressed their rage over the plots that the U.S.A. had brought to existence against their countries. They told me about numerous events in which their people suffered

Samih Masoud

greatly. I had heard of none of those stories before, because they were being overlooked due to the extent of time that had passed since their occurrences.

Antonio of Bethlehem

Chapter Twenty-Four

Antonio of Bethlehem

Samih Masoud

In the mid-1950s, the opposition fire in Colombia broke out after the conservative party won the parliamentary elections. This situation soon turned into a political strife, encountered by all the parties. At nighttime, protesters filled Bogotá's streets, as the unified voices of the people were strong. Over time, these voices became a part of the night.

The army interfered and military officers took over the government. They declared martial law and dismantled all the opposing parties, particularly the leftist ones. As a result, they were forced to work underground.

The number of imprisoned people increased fast. In fact, in a short period of time, the country turned into a huge prison cell where military officers were watching every step of the people. Being jailed for the sake of my country brought my inner light back to me. During the interrogation, I was happy to admit my membership in the Socialist Party. I did not betray my comrades and resisted all questioning about their names. Instead of addressing the questions of the interrogators, I talked about my familiarity with Palestine and my Arabic origin. I was not looking for any gain whatsoever.

I was kept in prison for several months, during which period I was treated inhumanely. I took refuge in the silence of my cell. No contact with the rest of the prisoners was allowed. One morning, which I shall never forget, I received my release order. I was joyful, because freedom is the most vital aspect of life.

I walked proudly to the prison gate where I was greeted by a large crowd of my party's members. Though with difficulty, I was able to walk to them. In that moment, I realized once again the importance of my comrades. The pouring of camaraderie I felt in their presence amazed me.

Antonio of Bethlehem

One day after being released from prison – the year was 1952, I took a few journals with me and went to a café near The Bolivar Square where I used to sit before. I sat up front and started sipping my coffee while I looked through my reading materials. I first paged through *The Jerusalem Post* that a friend from Bethlehem who lives in Chile had sent to me during my imprisonment. It was the same newspaper that was called *The Palestine Post*. The name was changed after the Jewish state was declared. It continued being published in English.

I read a few articles by Jewish writers who wrote with pride about the establishment of their state. They were ignoring the savage atrocities their forces committed against civilians, the uprooting of about a million Palestinians and the destruction of hundreds of Palestinian villages in a systematic way as part of an ethnic cleansing campaign to keep a Jewish majority in the occupied Palestine.

What the Jews achieved with the support of Britain and the USA had increased their power and enabled them to re-write history in a denial of the destruction and bloodshed they created and the crimes they committed against the Palestinian people.

I am not interested in what they have achieved now. I am interested in tomorrow's windstorm harvests. That is why I shall keep my dream alive and have it guide me anew with determination to the battlefield, so that I can sacrifice myself while lighting the candles of Bethlehem once again.

I looked through the last issue of *Life Magazine* next. The picture of the Colombian coup leader was on the cover, with a highlight on his fame among American lobbyists. I ended up also reading an extensive report on the role Colombia's new military government played in silencing the voices of the leftist parties and its inclination toward establishing strong relations with the USA.

My heart started to beat faster as I read the last words. I wondered if they were lies and only describing the vanity and desire to build an empire here with the help of American trans-continental companies.

Within one hour, I stopped reading and began to look around idly. A man suddenly appeared in front of me. He greeted me and asked me politely the best way to Monserrate. I gave him the directions. He was from Argentina, traveling with a friend in South American countries to learn about the state they are in. I invited him to have Colombian coffee with me. He agreed, and we introduced ourselves to each other. His name was Ernesto Guevara. This year was his last studying medicine at the Buenos Aires University.

He then waved to a man standing near the café's entrance and asked him to join us. His friend responded positively and introduced himself. Alberto Granado was also from Argentina and had a master's degree in biochemistry. They were on a motorcycle tour of South American countries. When their motorcycle broke down, they had to resort to other means of transport between the various villages and cities.

As we were drinking our coffee, Ernesto took a peek at the journals I had with me and asked: "Do you speak English?" "Yes," I said, "because I want to know the crimes committed by the USA against humanity in general and against South America in particular." He seemed pleased with my answer. We apparently shared the same thoughts. His words about the conspiracies plotted by the USA against South American countries sounded lovely to me. He also expressed his contempt to the savage capitalism that was bound to increase the hardship the working class presently endures by forcing them to a socially lower status.

I nodded my head in agreement. His view was in harmony with leftist theories: in favor of the oppressed people, trying to improve their living standards on a social, economic and political level. His words stirred something inside me. I took a deep breath and said enthusiastically: "I have the same thoughts on this matter. I believed in them since I was young, since the first time I began to notice certain realities around me."

His response was encouraging: "We are comrades in the same humanistic thought that I hope to turn into action for the sake of our helpless people."

Ernesto looked at an Arabic journal in front of me and asked: "Do you speak Arabic too?"

"Yes, I learned it in the past few years because it's the language of my ancestors." My answer took both men by surprise. Alberto asked: "From which Arabic country are your ancestors?" "Palestine," I replied. Ernesto had another question: "Have you been to Palestine?" "I have not only been there, but also fought for its liberation."

I told them in detail my involvement with the Palestinian resistance movement. They listened attentively.

Ernesto remarked: "In that case, you're an international fighter for the sake of freedom. I'm pleased to meet you!" Alberto reacted with the same enthusiasm. Embarrassed, I kept silent for a few minutes, then changed the subject: "It's time for you to get to know our lovely Monserrate!"

Samih Masoud

The three of us took a bus to Bogotá's famous high mountain. The long winding road that led us there offered us captivating views.

I noticed that Ernesto was writing down the entire time. After wiping off a few drops of sweat from his forehead, he said to me that time was passing by quickly and that he needed to record a lot of information in his daily journal before he went on his way to a new destination tomorrow.

Antonio of Bethlehem

Chapter

Twenty-Five

… Antonio of Bethlehem

Samih Masoud

The bus stopped at the feet of Monserrate. We walked to its peak where tourists usually gather. We enjoyed the panoramic view of Bogotá in its indescribably charming visual offerings. It was as if the city was waving at us in the horizon, as if it was a mere stone-throw away. We stayed there for a while before we began to explore around.

After a good amount of walking, it felt good to reach the Simon Bolivar Museum, which was originally Bolivar's palace. We could easily see that the great leader had many achievements. Historical reminders of the battles he had gone through all his life to attain independence for South America and enable its countries an everlasting unity were everywhere to see there.

After we left the museum, we took a nearby street to a restaurant for a late lunch. While we ate, we discussed many subjects; mostly though, the Bolivarian revolution and its place in South American history.

Ernesto talked about the possibility of another revolt in order to eliminate all oppressive regimes and to achieve social justice for the oppressed. "How can we keep silent about oppression? We must have a revolution everywhere!"

"I agree with you," I said, "but to have a successful revolution, all progressive and leftist forces must act as one."

Ernesto continued to talk about the dire need for revolutionary initiatives and asked me about the events that surrounded the military coup in Colombia.

I explained to him the political background that had led to the military officers' oppressive policies. I also talked about the martial law which was a means for the oppressors to fill prisons with resistance fighters. He asked me if I was one of those prisoners.

Antonio of Bethlehem

"I was released from prison yesterday. It was the first time for me to be in jail."

Looking surprised, he observed: "You're a real fighter! I do hope I shall find my way to the roads of resistance like you." He then asked: "How did you endure prison life?"

I tensed up while I described to him the severe security measures and the savage treatment of prisoners that were almost impossible to endure: "Prisoners are kept in tight and dark cells where they lose touch with reality. The strong ones among them stay true to their principles and even die for them. That is how I was – indifferent to what the authorities inflicted upon me, no matter how inhumane their interrogation tactics were. I refused to cooperate with them against my party and my homeland."

After we left the restaurant, we went to the bus station and took the bus to Bogotá. When we arrived there, it was close to sunset. We went to the city center through the main street. We then came to an alley. The hotel where Ernesto and Alberto were staying was only a short distance away. Before we went our own ways, we agreed to meet at 10 o'clock the next morning in the café where we had first encountered one another.

The next morning, we found ourselves heavily engaged in a discussion of local and international news over Colombian coffee. I gave Ernesto a few copies of my articles that I had published before the military coup. He immediately opened his daily journal. I read a few pages of his notes and found out the reason for their trip. He was describing in detail his impressions of the various villages, cities, and people from different social classes they came in touch with. Some of the people they had met were South America's original inhabitants whose suffering started the moment the white man had arrived there.

I asked Ernesto: "What prompted your long trip through South American countries?"

"Discovery! I wanted to discover the places and people in their natural environment. I also wanted to see oppression firsthand and man's need for freedom."

Ernesto was talking with high emotion, especially about Kosko in Peru (a.k.a. Cuzco and Cusco), the Inka capital and one of the oldest continuously inhabited cities in the Western Hemisphere. He was fascinated by Kosko's past. Through a reflection on the present conditions, he chronologized the ethnic cleansing to which the white man subjected the original inhabitants. By doing so, he was underlining the fact that none of those atrocities had come to an end. He saw the evidence in the recent initiatives of the USA, a country that plunders South America by installing mercenaries to carry out its imperialist agenda.

Ernesto stressed how strongly their trip influenced his thought process, helping him develop into a revolutionary man, filled with a desire to liberate the people of South America for the good of all humanity. On account of his travels, he was able to realize how much closer he now was to a life of sacrifice for a revolution. He added that he would be happy to burn in its flames while breathing in the smell of gunpowder as a sign of a defeat for the enemy.

As Alberto was collecting his scattered thoughts, he uttered: "We packed up one morning in December of last year, 1951, and started our journey. Ernesto was different then. The poor conditions under which the original inhabitants were living affected him very much, along with the sight of an overwhelming flood of US companies and their strategies to simply make money and more money."

Ernesto agreed with his friend, "Yes, I have indeed changed significantly during our trip. I re-examined my past and have now no difficulty in choosing the path of resistance for the sake of humanity. My hope is to actively participate in actual battles in South America."

Alberto checked the time and reminded his friend: "It's time for us to go!" "Yes," Ernesto responded, "we must be on our way to Caracas."

They were going to work in a well-known Venezuelan medical center in Caracas. After finishing his last year in medical school, Ernesto would then leave for Buenos Aires.

We exchanged our addresses, and Ernesto promised to correspond with me so that we could continue to communicate to each other our thoughts about the problems of South America.

I felt sad that they had to leave. After they took off, I ran our conversations through my mind and concluded that Ernesto was on his way to become a revolutionary.

Chapter

Twenty-Six

# Antonio of Bethlehem

Samih Masoud

The military's influence continued to expand in Bogotá. Public protests were also spreading across the entire country. People were resisting the power of the military government which had connections to the CIA. The junta was responding to the protesters with bullets, filling Colombia with blood.

Political parties played a vital role in organizing public protests – irrespective of their different ideologies. My party had established solid contacts with all parties. I became a member of the committee that was responsible for organizing demonstrations and attacks which gained momentum with each passing day. I was very active in my role, and was therefore pursued by the security and intelligence services of the military.

While clashes continued to enfold in Bogotá, I regularly received letters from Khaled who helped me connect with my comrades in Palestine. I was still very sad for the fall of the Palestinian movement. Khaled wrote to me about the conditions of Palestinian immigrants, their forced travels into camps in many Arabic countries and the situation in Jerusalem. That city had now become a ghost town, as most of its inhabitants had left; in particular the rich who once lived in stately homes outside the old city wall. All this news stirred in me a deep sense of sorrow.

During that period of my life, I was highly interested in the events surrounding Palestine and Colombia, but also South America at large. Avidly, I was keeping up-to-date with the developments in those regions. Based on the level of my passion toward them, I made a list of the countries I felt the urge to stay connected to, focusing on the link between them, not on their differences. With time, I became more idealistic than ever before. I had come to the understanding that a revolutionary fighter had to be idealistic and a dreamer in order to effectuate a change in the actual reality toward justice and liberty.

I brought up this matter with my comrades. After lengthy discussions, we collectively concluded that our ideals were a critical part of the progression of our thoughts.

It was impossible to be dissatisfied with my party's decisions in its attempt to define the path for our resistance. I had written an article on this subject. In it, I had provided many facts that did not originate from any hearsay, but from my informative findings: a revolution's ideology does not overcome reality, but rather blends it with humane attributes.

At the time of the Colombian junta, I became more acutely aware of my idealism. The successful reforms in Guatemala, accomplished by President Jacob Arbenz Guzman, had given me a sharper insight. He was democratically elected and made those reforms under the persistent pressure of the masses. He distributed large areas of land among the peasants and turned other courageous reforms into reality, all of which were supported by the Guatemalans and national movements, especially by leftist parties.

The end result of President Guzman's achievements was the transformation of Guatemala into a model for revolutionaries in all the countries of South America. Hundreds of them mobilized to preserve the reforms and lent their support to the government against the US agenda. The US was always ready to fight regional resistance in order to serve its own economic interests. And those interests had been hurt by the reforms.

Samih Masoud

In 1954, I traveled to Guatemala where I joined the reformists as Guevara had also done. I met him there and we both lived in one of the centers designated to those who were arriving there from South American countries. We both participated in the nation-wide resistance.

One evening as Guevara and I were talking, he suddenly became silent. He was hardly able to breathe while he erratically tried to utter something. I was sure that he was having an asthma attack. He was known to have suffered from bronchial spasms in his early life. He immediately took his medicine and was feeling better. So, we both proceeded with our conversation. Our focus was on the losses the USA had suffered in Guatemala because of the national reforms. The American United Fruits Company was particularly hard-hit, as it used to dominate a vast area of land previously.

Guevara's voice pulled me out of my thoughts: "The USA will not keep quiet; it will return to its imperialist strategies and suppress the countries that behave against its will." He then spoke in a more serious tone: "Today, a detailed analysis from an important member of the local communist party was brought to my attention. The report indicated that the CIA was involved in a military coup to overthrow the current government and install one that will serve the USA interests."

I listened to Guevara intently and told him that I was not surprised with what I heard, because this tactic was what the USA had always used with other countries over the years. I added that confronting this renegade country was a must and that we have to ignite the resistance fire in all South American countries and stand against the savage US actions.

With time, indications of the expected coup became clearer. One morning, the coup indeed took place. A mercenary force invaded Guatemala via Honduras, and resistance was weak. Thus, the democratically elected president was overthrown and a military government was installed.

The Guatemalan experience came as a shock to all the members of the leftist movements. It was also a radical turning point in Guevara's life; for it transformed this young man who was only concerned with the poor living conditions of his people into a hardened and more passionate fighter on international platforms. From this point on, he was going to form a resistance movement with revolutionary targets to defeat American imperialism.

Guevara narrated to me the heroic actions of actual revolutionaries and the critical role they played in the gathering of the proletariat and the poor under the revolution's banner. Those heroes were successful in igniting the fire of the paramilitary and other armed combatants, in taking the enemy by surprise with their continuous strikes and in staying in hiding whenever a confrontation was too risky.

I knew that I was in the presence of a revolution leader who was completely different than the two I had met in Bogotá. He was indeed different! In one of our conversations, I confided in him: "I agree with you that revolution everywhere is the only solution. Before you, however, I used to believe in the revolutionary approach simply because I had fought in Palestine." When he kept silent, I raised a question: "What's our next step after the Guatemalan resistance?" With utmost enthusiasm in his voice, he answered: "Cuba!"

Guevara explained the importance of a Cuban revolution. As a follower of the events in Cuba, I mentioned the July 26 Revolution which failed in its attack on The Moncada Barracks. That revolution's leader, Fidel Castro, was now in Batista's prison in Santiago di Cuba, and Castro's forces had been disassembled while some of his comrades were living in exile outside Cuba.

Guevara comforted me by addressing my concerns. Castro's comrades were now living in Mexico, getting organized to overthrow Batista, and had good chances for a success after their previously failed attempt.

I had actually heard about Castro's comrades and their capability to confront Batista's oppressive regime and tyrannical forces. Guevara shouted: "We must join them!"

Without hesitation, I agreed with Guevara. We decided to immediately connect with the revolutionaries in Mexico. We had not met any of them before. We knew them only through the news.

Antonio of Bethlehem

Chapter

Twenty-Seven

Antonio of Bethlehem

Samih Masoud

On a spring day, I woke up early and met with Guevara. He introduced me to three men from the Guatemalan resistance movement. We left the secret place where we had been staying during the days after the military coup. We went towards a hill and sat under a tree.

One of the three men sat a little far from us. His name was Manuel. He opened a hand bag he was carrying. I wondered what was in it. He took out two passports. He was quiet as he glanced at them. Then he looked at us and said in a serious tone: "The revolution leaders are keen on providing all the fighters with fake passports. Your pictures will be taken upon your arrival. My two comrades and I will accompany you to our border with Mexico. There will be a car waiting for us in a nearby village." He gave Guevara and me our new passports. Shortly after we arrived in the village of Manuel's mention, a small pickup appeared. We drove to the Mexican border.

We were silent throughout the ride. We left the car near a Mexican police station. Manuel wished us good luck and left with his two comrades. Guevara and I went through passport control. The formalities to enter Mexico were finished quickly. We took a cab to Guadalajara. From there, we left for the capital with public transportation. Guevara was eager to talk with the passengers and asked them many questions about their country. He told them about the brotherhood between all South American people.

The conversation turned rather colorful when citing poetry and singing were added to it. We all chanted songs, showing feelings uninhibitedly. They were songs popular in all the countries of South America, songs that made one feel as if the entire continent was one country.

Antonio of Bethlehem

Guevara said: "You're my brothers in one homeland that we control with our own sovereignty." The passengers understood his symbolism well. They clapped enthusiastically.

When we arrived in the capital, we expressed our goodbyes with hugs. I turned to Guevara to say: "These are the people who give the revolution its life." His response was full of fervor: "They are our comrades!"

Guevara went to one of his friends while I stayed with a Mexican friend whom I had known during his college years in Bogotá. After a short while, however, I got sick and had to stay in bed. Guevara attended to me and brought me the news about Cuba.

After my health was restored, we met at a café where he was surrounded by many leftists. I noticed him looking around as if he was expecting someone. He then came over to me and whispered: "I've met a great Cuban fighter!" I shouted in excitement: "When?" He said: "Yesterday!" He introduced me to three of his comrades who were leaders in the July 26 Movement. They were very hopeful about creating a better future for their homeland which had been under a dictatorship. Guevara then told me that their initiative started as a reaction to Batista's coup. Fidel Castro had formed a combatant force and attacked the Moncada Barracks in Santiago de Cuba. The attack resulted in the death of a number of Castro's followers and his arrest. I asked Guevara how he discovered the fighters whom I had just met. "They are preparing for a courageous uprising in

Samih Masoud

Cuba. I expect that it is going to have a great impact on the political reality in all South American countries."

A few days later, Mexican newspapers wrote that Fidel Castro was released from prison and exiled to Mexico. Guevara met him when he arrived in the capital. Later on, Guevara invited me to a special meeting on a day in 1955. The meeting was held in an old house that belonged to the Banijas, a Mexican family. It was located near the Centro Historico quarter, where the relics of the Aztec civilization were found.

I met many Cuban fighters. Discussions were focused on the problems in our continent at large and on the necessary efforts and sacrifices to be made in order to ignite a revolution against reactionary regimes everywhere.

After a few days, Guevara invited me to another meeting; this time, in a farm in a suburb of Mexico City. Fidel Castro headed the meeting, and the planning for the July 26 Movement was done in the presence of a few Cuban revolutionaries in exile.

Fidel Castro was surrounded by five people, one of them was his brother Raul. Guevara introduced me as an international fighter with experiences in resistance movements in Palestine and Guatemala. I explained that my bond to Colombia and the rest of the South American countries was as strong as my tie to Palestine. I stressed the fact that I was willing to die for Cuba's sake.

I told them in detail about my involvement with the resistance movements in the past. Castro praised me. His wish for me to train new fighters for guerilla warfare when we go to Cuba to revive the revolution caught me by surprise. Happy to know his confidence in me, I gave him

Antonio of Bethlehem

my word: "I'm at your disposal. I'm ready to join the Cuban revolution until victory is achieved."

Preparations to obtain the necessary equipment and supplies for the return of the revolutionaries to Cuba proceeded in Mexico. Fidel and Raul Castro were highly active. Guevara was always with them. They were all passionately devoted to the revolution. Unfortunately, information about their whereabouts was discovered by Mexico's intelligence service, which led to their arrests. They were put in a cell. We had to put a hold on our preparations until they were released. After this incident, we took more effective measures to keep away from the surveillance of the intelligence services.

In the meantime, Castro met a Mexican arms dealer, Dell Condi, who cherished Castro's ideology. Thus, they became friends and combined their efforts. Dell Condi provided Castro with arms and military equipment, all of which were necessary means for the revolution. He also provided him with a boat, called "Granma", which was to be used for our trip to Cuba. "Granma" was purchased from an American by the name of Robert Erickson.

The boat was in a very bad condition. Dell Condi needed a long time to fix it. When it was ready, the trip to Cuba was in the offing.

Chapter Twenty-Eight

Antonio of Bethlehem

Samih Masoud

It was two o'clock in the morning on November 25, 1956 when I arrived with a number of my comrades at the Mexican port Tuxpan. On one of the docks, Fidel, Raul, Guevara and the rest of the comrades were waiting for us. We were a small group of 82 people. We all stood near "Granma", a blue boat. I was astonished to see how small it was. Then I remembered Dell Condi's words to Fidel: "The boat is small and very old and it won't take these many men. It can only carry twenty people."

Fidel had thanked him for his warning but explained to him with a smile that he had heard it before; that they would still sail in this boat as planned, and that they will endure the difficulties together.

It was time to sail. We all got into the boat, staying close to one another, and left the harbor keeping all the lights off. Dell Condi was on the dock, waving at us. After "Granma" was out of sight from the harbor, we turned on the lights. The boat's speed has gradually increased. We sailed near the shore at first, then into the middle of the sea. There were strong winds, and we all got seasick as the boat was swaying like a feather inside the turbulent waves. In fact, it felt like she was about to sink.

I was standing near Guevara and said to him with conviction, "Death is death whether in the sea or on land!" He spoke in a serious tone: "What we look for is death in the battle field. Our desired freedom as well as our beliefs will flourish there."

I kept watching the boat's course while death accompanied her. The voices of my comrades comforted me. They were singing the Cuban national anthem and the landmark song of the July 26 Movement. They were chanting "Cuba" in repetition, which stirred in me the revolutionary flame anew.

Castro was not far from me when he cited a poem to Guevara. He told him that it belonged to the Cuban poet José Martí whose deliberations had prompted the Cuban revolution before his death in 1895. Castro also told Guevara that José Martí was his source of inspiration.

On the evening of our first day of sailing, the sun was about to set, casting its rays upon the sea and leaving glowing sparkles on the waves. The boat was shaking violently as she moved up and down, and we were being thrown around in all directions. As the night fell and I was looking at the horizon, my seasickness got worse. I tried to concentrate on the boat's route. We crossed the Mexico Bay and the Caribbean Sea and then took a sharp turn south of Cuba, sailing on the Jamaican coast and passing by the Cayman Islands.

A week later, I noticed lights faraway that became more and more distinct as the boat kept sailing. We were moving towards land. Castro shouted at the top of his lungs: "Comrades, we're near Cuba!" All of us released our emotions. Our boat set anchor at Playa Las Coloradas, far away from any military surveillance.

On the 2nd of December in 1956, we set foot in Cuba. We walked through sugarcane fields, carrying our combat equipment on our backs. We then ascended to a nearby forest where we stopped. We rested under the shades of the trees, as the long trip had exhausted all of us.

After one whole day of rest, we gathered around Fidel. He declared in a short speech that we were at the first stage of the revolution and that we must be ready to confront

Batista's army. We were going to confront that army with our small group.

Fidel turned to me and said, "I told you in Mexico that you would be responsible for training the fighters on all the special maneuvers of guerilla warfare." As thoughts were racing through my head, I responded with confidence: "I'm ready to do this job the best I can!"

We were exploring our surroundings the next day when were ambushed by Batista's soldiers. We fought courageously but we unfortunately lost many of our comrades. Only ten of us were still alive, to include Fidel, Guevara, Raul and Camilo.

The army attack drew Cubans to the revolution. Volunteers came from many different regions but from the countryside in particular, either individually or in groups. Because of the great number of volunteers, a unit was formed for the trainees. The revolutionary forces were thus able to increase their power and had many victories in the cities which weakened the Batista regime and his army. What was most distinctly noted in that stage of the revolution was the rise of Guevara's fame as "Che". Fidel promoted him to the position of the second commander for what he had achieved in our combats.

In light of these new developments, Guevara suggested a new strategy. He called for a battle in the main cities. His objective was to remove Batista and his cabinet and install a rule accepted by the people, which was to be mainly linked to the proletarian class. Based on this approach, our forces were sectioned systematically into groups. Fidel Castro led a group to Santiago de Cuba in the southeastern side of the island and was able to liberate it as well as other cities. Another group, led by Che Guevara and in which I was a fighter, took control of the mountainous Las Mercedes, Las Filas, Cabayguan, Guayus and other cities and villages.

The victories of Guevara's group emerged in a short period of time yielding to a historical triumph for the revolutionary forces: Santa Clara was liberated on the Christmas Eve of 1958. A few days after the city's liberation, Batista escaped to Portugal. On the 1st day of January 1959 then, Castro declared in Santiago de Cuba the absolute success of the revolution throughout Cuba.

The next day, Guevara arrived in Havana to take control of the city. Six days later, Fidel arrived there victoriously and was received by the city's population in a passionate embrace. The revolutionary anthem could be heard from everywhere as the revolution forces roamed throughout the city. The island had gained historical prominence in the world for its victorious revolutions.

Days went by with many memorable moments, rich also in their spiritual giving. I am thrilled whenever I think of all the circumstances and occurrences that led to a unique revolution; a revolution that South American people took possession of in their determination to see the liberation of their countries from the US hegemony.

Chapter

Twenty-Nine

Antonio of Bethlehem

Samih Masoud

I heard Castro repeating a phrase in all of his public speeches – to the effect that 'the real revolution starts after a victory'. He would evidence the progresses made after the revolution, offer an analytical insight, and therefore, talk for hours.

As far as efforts to rebuild the cities, Castro had constructive proposals. His innovative ideas and plans started to be heard all over Cuba. Every initiative was being completed according to the "Sierra Maestra" declaration. The first steps included the confiscation of private properties, nationalization of public services and adoption of a socialist system for all walks of life.

In the political arena, Cuba's relationship with the Soviet Union was strengthened thanks to the fact that the July 26 Movement had merged with the Cuban Communist Party. What followed was the complete integration of socialist countries on all grounds.

On those days, it felt like as if even the horizon was covered with the images of the rebuilding projects. Che Guevara held many ministerial positions in the fields of industry, economics and central banking. In his multi-faceted capacity, he offered extensive guidance which was critical for the revolution's success in its first years.

Che also joined revolutionary movements abroad. He was given many tasks that he always fulfilled masterfully, making an impact on the platform of the United Nations and a multitude of conferences across the globe. As a delegate of the Cuban government, he visited a number of Arabic cities, including Cairo, Algiers and Gaza. Wherever he went, he was received with a most genial welcome for his international leadership.

I met with him after his visit to Gaza. He spoke to me about the Palestinian cause and his sorrow over the tragedy of the Palestinian refugees. They had been forced to leave their cities and villages because of the terrorist Zionist attacks and had to live in camps that were deprived of the basic needs to sustain a life.

What he had seen and heard during his visits to many countries had affected Che deeply. At that stage of his life, he concentrated his efforts to contribute to the intellectual advancements of the people everywhere. He was acutely aware that there were necessary changes to be made for the sake of humanity at large. Through his participation in worldwide revolutions, he was able to help the people materialize the needed changes with actual results. He thus proved that wiping out all forms of oppression and despotism was a must everywhere.

Che announced a worldwide revolution as he was getting ready for it. He left Havana to join the war in East Congo. There, he led a military campaign of 100 fighters who were assembled from the guerilla forces of the Cuban war. The battles lasted for 7 months and ended with failure, an outcome that diminished Che's African dream. Losing in the war in East Congo, however, did not eradicate Cuba's important position in the African continent. Cuba continued to offer its political and military support to many movements and governments in various parts of Africa, particularly in Angola and South Africa.

A multitude of events occurred after successful revolutions – whether their location was Cuba, Africa or South America. A status was designed for me in the Cuban army so that I could document the revolutionary history. This responsibility was in sync with my specialty in political history as well as my personal convictions.

To complete one of my responsibilities I chronicled the significant achievements of revolutions. This task encompassed the documentation of the various events from the time of the Cuban revolution's conception in Mexico City to the phase of the guerilla warfare in the mountains of Sierra Maestra and in big cities. That revolution was, after all, crowned in triumph, resulting in the removal of Batista's regime and the start of a people's rule in Cuba.

I lent special attention to "Granma" in my documentation. The boat was kept in a barrack after going through a necessary maintenance. I went to that barrack often to see our boat. I always found tranquility around it. I would reminisce about our risky trip, throughout which waves kept pounding that small vessel while sunrays traveled in through the tiny windows. Our trip in that boat was unforgettable.

I had requested for "Granma" to be kept in a museum specifically designed for the revolution. My thinking was that its visibility would serve as a constant reminder to Cubans for generations to come. It would remind them of a historical trip that Fidel Castro, Che Guevara and their comrades had taken to Cuba to start the revolution.

In addition to my official work in the army, I was keen on getting acquainted with Havana, especially its old part. I walked for long hours on alleys and winding, stone-paved streets, stopping in front of the many buildings that displayed the Andalusian architectural style as influenced by Granada and Cordova.

I also connected to people of Arabic origin, through whom I discovered a small Palestinian community. I was

Antonio of Bethlehem

thrilled to find out that three individuals among them were from Jerusalem. My conversation with them awakened my memories of Palestine. I got to know their families and wandered through the old city with them. I also learned about the University of Havana in the Vedado district. It was founded in 1728. It is considered one of the oldest universities in South America. Then I discovered the Seville Hotel with its Andalusian columns and arches and the historical Libri Hotel that was Castro's meeting place after the revolution. The latter is an important part of Havana's heritage due to its age, but also because it offers valuable information about the Cuban revolution.

I had the chance to see Paseo del Prado, the most beautiful alley in Havana. It is located near the old city and is famous with its tall trees surrounding it, the marble seats on its sidewalks and the lion statues and flower pots adorning the balconies of old houses – all of which are etched in the collective Cuban memory. I sat together with my Palestinian acquaintances near the marble columns, taking in the view of the alley that in the past was the most important place for Havana's rich.

I visited the Great Havana Theatre, Grand Theatro di la Havana, which is one of the largest theaters in the world. It was constructed 250 years ago with the architectural touches of the Parque. Cultural organizations had decided to make it the home for the national Cuban ballet that rivals world's greatest ballet centers. The Cuban ballet dancers are some of the best known across the globe.

I have also familiarized myself with the Parque Central, finding myself in front of El Capitolio Nacional de La Habana with its large dome. In its architectural style, that structure looks a lot like the famous U.S. Capitol Building. I was stunned by the size of the dome of El Capitolio Nacional de La Habana. It is said that it is visible from all over Havana. What makes it stand out are the ornamental ledges of various shapes on its façade. The Havana Capitol was used as a government building before the revolution.

The famous El Floridita Café, built in 1817 and as such, one of Havana's historical landmarks, was located in front of El Capitolio Nacional de La Habana. The café's overall design may be characterized as one of exceptional beauty and artistry. I was told that it was a favorite destination for the famous American writer Ernest Hemingway. When he had lived in Cuba for a long time, he was there on a regular basis. Hemingway had supported the Cuban revolution and met Castro after his victory.

Having heard these specifics about Hemingway, I wanted to visit the great writer's house. One of my Palestinian friends had a car. So, we went to Finca la Vigia, a village near Havana where the house was. We arrived at the address, left the car in a farm full of tropical trees, and walked slowly to a high hill near the Caribbean Sea. We toured Hemingway's house. It was full of books on large bookshelves, with heads of wild animals mounted above them. The writer himself had hunted those animals as he had a special love for hunting.

I learned from the guide in the house that Hemingway had written his famous novel, *The Old Man and the Sea* in 1951 in this house. For that novel, he had received the 1954 Nobel Prize for Literature as well as the Pulitzer Prize for his groundbreaking style in the genre. His inspiration came from his friend, the Cuban fisherman Georgio Fuentos whom Hemingway had met in 1928. Hemingway had given his protagonist the name "Santiago", who was an old Cuban fisherman fishing at Gold Stream Bay. The writer's love for fishing thus came to the foreground.

I continued to meet the members of Havana's Palestinian community in their homes where we conversed upon many subjects related to Palestine. I loved our conversations about our homeland and seeing that their physical distance from it did not make them forget their roots. One of them, Carlos, was well aware of the Palestinian Nakba. He talked about it in a highly informed manner. He also spoke of the Palestinian refugees and the camps where the refugees were forced to live in, despite the lack of even the basic necessities.

One day, I was in Carlos' home. He told me how Algeria became highly interested in the Palestinian problem after the victory of the Algerian revolution. He came closer to me as if he wanted to share with me a secret: "Together with Syria and Egypt, Algeria is preparing to liberate Palestine from the Zionist claws. There are also some active Palestinian forces working seriously on a new Palestinian revolution."

I felt very happy to hear what Carlos had confided in me. I immediately shared with him my stance: "I will join them at the time of the first revolutionary spark."

Chapter

Thirty

Antonio of Bethlehem

Samih Masoud

One day, I met with Che in his office in an old fortress near Havana Bay. I found him standing by a window looking at the sea. I stood beside him and asked: "Do you remember our sea trip on 'Granma'?"

"How can I forget it?" he answered.

Scenes of the past came to life in his emotion-laden words. Che reminisced about our many fallen comrades. His great sorrow over the loss of his comrade Camilo Sinfigos resurfaced. After our victory, Camilo's plane had crashed and he was lost in the sea. That memory was etched in the depth of his heart. He repeatedly mentioned it in his private and public speeches.

We talked extensively about Camilo. Che said somberly, "I'm sorry for what happened to Camilo. I was very sad when he died. I still cannot believe that he is dead. I always look at the sea from here and wait for the waves to bring him back."

We talked in sadness about the notable conducts of our great comrade Camilo. He was one of the key figures in the Cuban revolution, working side by side with Fidel Castro, Che Guevara, Jwan Almida and Raul Castro. He was 27 when he was killed. As I mentioned before, his plane had crashed and fell into the Atlantic Ocean a few months after the revolution was declared a victory. His body was never found. Every year on the day of his death, flowers are spread into the ocean as he is being remembered as a revolutionary legend. His face dons the Cuban currency of 40 pesos. Che had named one of his sons after him.

Che took the last sip of his coffee, pressed on his temples and said, "For the sake of Camilo, I want to ignite a worldwide revolution." I asked him, "Are conditions suitable for that initiative, considering your experience in

Antonio of Bethlehem

Africa, especially in Congo where the guerillas were hit severely?" He answered with conviction: "We must learn from our mistakes and prepare accordingly. We must start with our continent but through new strategies. We must defeat American imperialism and rid our countries of oppressive rulers and traitors."

Che talked about the details of his plans, which reflected the afterthoughts he must have had following his African experience. He began to smoke a Cuban cigar, which he loved, and asked, "Will you stand by me in the forthcoming guerilla war?" "Of course," I answered, "without any hesitation!" Pleased with my response, he said, "We'll take the first step soon!"

I met with him many times after that day and came to know that Bolivia was going to be the next destination for our guerilla warfare. He told me that the Bolivian forests were an outward indication of providing the necessary ground for a successful revolution. He was anticipating that it would quickly spread to many South American countries from there.

I still remember those moments in Che's office vividly and think of them often.

At a later date, Che called for a meeting in his office, which I attended with a group of about 20 comrades. Their comments showed me that they too were aware of his plans for a worldwide revolution and that they too were ready to give up their lives for its sake.

Che read us the details of the executive plan to get to Bolivia. He said that we will assemble in an abandoned farm, which was surrounded by forests. He showed its location on the map, specifying that it was situated a few meters from Incahuasi, with a small river welling out from it.

Fake passports were distributed to the group. We received instructions to follow the identified safe passage to Bolivia. Che had designated an approximate meeting time and was particularly meticulous about stressing the importance of us being camouflaged at all times.

Antonio of Bethlehem

Chapter

Thirty-One

Antonio of Bethlehem

Samih Masoud

In the afternoon of November 7, 1966, our group arrived in Bolivia. Che held the first meeting in the farm. He started his speech in a poetic way as he welcomed us for living once again in the forests. He repeated the reason behind his choice to begin our guerilla warfare in that location: all indications pointed to its opportune ground for a victory.

Che's speech was inspirational in its stress on hope in our dire circumstances. He was convinced that we were on the right path and that opportunities were there for us to achieve our goals and defeat the imperialist American forces.

We built our camp on a small plateau near the farm. Then we started to establish the necessary communications to attract peasants, laborers and oppressed people to our side. Unfortunately, there was minimal response. Even the Bolivian Communist Party, leftist and nationalist parties and labor syndicates refused to collaborate with us. Our doubts grew when the potential of success was concerned. I personally felt that we were in danger. It was as if the silence of the forest was announcing so.

I met with Che alone when we were at Ayacucho. I told him about my concerns regarding that which was taking place around us. He did not share the same worries. On the contrary, he questioned them in an attempt to boast my morale. No matter what he said, I was unable to shake off the thoughts that were troubling me. The feeling that we were throwing ourselves into an all-consuming fire with our small number of men and meager means would not leave me in peace. Our current circumstances were in stark contrast to our experience in Cuba when the July 26 Movement had attracted a great number of people.

Antonio of Bethlehem

What affected my poor state of mind even more was the apprehension of the French leftist thinker Regis Dupré and his torture in a prison in Camiri. During his interrogation by the Bolivian security apparatus, he had confessed that Che was the one leading the guerilla warfare in the Bolivian forests. At the same time, three of our comrades had also confessed under torture. The Bolivian Army knew where Che was, and had therefore intensified their search for him and his revolutionary group.

On the 5th day of June 1967, one comrade informed me that the Bolivian radio stations were talking about a war in the Middle East. I immediately turned on my transistor radio, caught a strong enough signal from a nearby Bolivian radio tower and listened to the news. I listened to the news for six days. When the war in the Middle East came to an end, three Arabic countries had lost and Israel had occupied a vast area of land; West Bank, Sinai and the Golan Heights, to be specific.

I was extremely sad because Israel had control over all of Palestine, including East Jerusalem as well as Bethlehem. The outcome of that war was a great shock to me; a shock that I had never experienced before. I was severely depressed. I felt lost and was unable to bear the pains that had befallen me. I desperately searched for myself, only to see myself disappear between Colombia, Cuba and Palestine. Oh Palestine, the land of my ancestors!

A short time after the June War, the international news agencies began to announce that Palestinian fidayeen movements were executing military operations against Israel. Those initiatives became well-known for their use of new maneuvers in guerrilla warfare. They had camps in some Arabic countries neighboring Palestine where their forces were being trained. On account of their brave confrontations with Israel, those fighters became heroes in people's eyes.

I decided to travel to the Middle East to join this new wave of Palestinian resistance. I spoke ardently to Che about my intent. Without any hesitation, he welcomed my decision: "Your determination is proof that we made the right choice to ignite a worldwide revolution." Passionately, he wished me good luck. I became quite emotional when we hugged and while I bid farewell to my comrades. Many memories rushed to my head as I thought of everything we went through in Cuba.

I left for the Chilean border for passport control. Then I went to the capital, Santiago. I walked the distance between the train station and the Palestinian Sports Club. Luckily, I ran into two friends from the Palestinian community there. I had met them during my previous visits. We had a long talk about the defeat of the six-day war. I told them about my plan to participate in the new resistance movement in Palestine. They encouraged me wholeheartedly and provided me with plane tickets to get to the fidayeen camps. They laid out my travel destinations for me: Madrid, Beirut and Amman.

The next morning, two friends took me to the airport. After a long hiatus, my return to Palestine had begun.

Antonio of Bethlehem

Chapter

Thirty-Two

Antonio of Bethlehem

Samih Masoud

I arrived in Amman on July 20, 1967. There, I received information about the Palestinian fidayeen. I went to one of the designated offices where I have been informed about the structure of those fighter groups. They had bases in Valley Al Aghwar, which is adjacent to River Jordan, and had initiated the Palestinian revolution with a highly successful outcome. I was happy to hear about their achievements but also to find out the new face of the guerilla warfare.

I wanted to know more about one of the leftist factions. I met with a number of its leaders and told them about my gratitude for their commitment to fight against oppression and injustice. I also told them about my involvement in resistance movements in Palestine, Cuba and other countries. We conversed for a long time. I shared with them my insights, all of which were based on my previous experiences.

I continued to meet other fidayeen in Valley Al Aghwar, but also at the al-Hussein refugee camp. My connection to those groups was based on our common goals and our efforts to achieve those goals, and not on some useless theoretical contemplations. With the passage of time, I became more and more attached to these resistance groups until one day I joined them officially. I was excited to be with them in that camp. From there, I could see with my naked eyes the banana orchards in Areeha (Jericho) and the peaks of the mountains around Jerusalem. I was sad for being unable to go there.

One morning as I was preoccupied looking at the horizon, one of our comrades asked me: "Have you heard the latest news about Che Guevara?" With trepidation, I answered, "No." He said that Che was arrested by the CIA agents. I was badly shaken up by this news. I felt as if everything around me was collapsing. I turned on my transistor radio and started listening to the news. He was arrested in Quebrada de Coro, moved to a school in the village of La Herrera and was to be executed on November 9, 1967. I was in a state of hopeless despair.

Newspapers from all around the world printed Che Guevara's pictures after his execution. Many commentaries donned those papers where he was portrayed as a saint because of his incessant resistance against oppression and imperialism.

A Palestinian revolution faction invited me to give a eulogy in honor of Che's martyrdom. Though I was grieving inconsolably, I accepted the invitation. In my eulogy, I talked about the various stages of his lifelong dedication to revolutions that he had carried out as great and small victories. I also talked about his vital role in the victorious Santa Clara battle, a guerilla warfare that had opened the doors of victory for the Cuban revolution. Other comrades also honored Che in their speeches, stressing the facts that his political consciousness always sided with the oppressed and that he took their problems as his own, fighting for their sake.

Che gave his life to the last battle he had waged together with his comrades in the forests of Bolivia.

I continued to stay in Valley Al Aghwar, lucky to join the al-Karama battle where the Jordanian army fought alongside the fidayeen against the Israeli army. It was the first time that the Arabs defeated the so-called non-defeated army. This battle reminded me of those in which I participated in Cuba.

Through the al-Karama battle, I saw firsthand the Jordanian military strategy. As the fidayeen talked openly about their experiences in the battle, I also learned much from them. I felt fortunate to be with them.

After the al-Karama battle, the comrade in charge of the camp in Al Aghwar asked me to get ready for a round of visits to Syria and Lebanon. The plan was for me to see the conditions of the Palestinian refugees there in order to make a plan to draw them into the revolution. The al-Karama battle had increased the credibility of the fidayeen in the eyes of many, getting the attention of the masses in the refugee camps.

I did my work according to the plan. As I was ready to leave Beirut for Amman, I met by chance a relative of mine, Nassri, whom I had seen in Amman. He invited me to Kuwait where he lived and worked. He praised Kuwait because it had always supported the fidayeen initiatives. I was pleased to hear what he added to his invitation: "You can meet your old friend Fadhel Rasheed, your comrade in the Holy Jihad Army. He also lives and works in Kuwait." Nassri told me that he meets Fadhel every now and then. He had heard a lot from him about the al-Qastal battle and the explosion of the Jewish Agency.

Excitement grew in me as I listened to Nassri's words which reminded me of the battles I had joined in the past. I accepted his invitation enthusiastically. He made all the arrangements for my visit. Together, we went to the Beirut airport and took a plane to Kuwait.

Antonio of Bethlehem

Chapter

Thirty-Three

Antonio of Bethlehem

Samih Masoud

In the evening of a day in July 1969, our plane landed in Kuwait. We went to Hawalli where he lived and worked. Once in his home, where I had been before, he gave me a comfortable room to settle in throughout my visit. He said with a smile: "You will stay with us at least for two weeks." "But that's a long time." I said. He was quick to respond, "No arguments!" Our familial relationship and our deep roots in Bethlehem became the subject of our many conversations. He seemed especially passionate when he talked about Palestine.

In the next days, Nassri introduced me to some of our relatives, also living in Kuwait. One morning, I met with my friend Fadhel Rasheed, the Iraqi officer who was the right hand of the commander of the Holy Jihad Army. We talked for a long time about our battles in Palestine and reminisced about our comrades-in-arms.

Fadhel and I continued many of our conversations in Nassri's home. We also roamed the city many times. He showed me its neighborhoods and markets. We met some Palestinians at the al-Mubarakiyya Market, in the Al Safa Square, and on various streets. I noticed that special boxes were set up to collect contributions for the fidayeen. Collections were also stored in business centers, cafés and on major streets.

One day, I had an interesting time with an Egyptian journalist who came with his friend to Nassri's home. I gave a long interview, answering his many questions about my past. I shared with him many memories that were filled with incidents and stories. After three days, the interview was published in the Kuwaiti newspaper, *al-Hadaf*. My criticism of tyranny, oppression and imperialism was printed in big letters. The details of my active involvement with the resistance movements in Palestine and Cuba were printed in color and designated to a special column.

After that interview, I heeded the encouragement I received from Fadhel. He had suggested that I delve into my memory to rediscover myself during various times and in different places. I worked painstakingly on recording them over the next ten days in pure self-examination. It is my life story that I molded into a tangible form in my own voice.

I gave the tapes to Fadhel. He promised me that he would publish them in a book, adding that he was adamant about his intent. I watched him looking at the tapes in gratitude. I had given him an important part of my life.

The Author's Epilogue

Antonio of Bethlehem

Samih Masoud

Three days after Fadhel received the recordings, Antonio took his last breath. The clock of death had rung for this eminent fighter on the 4th of August of the year 1969 in Kuwait. He was 60 years old.

Befitting the magnitude of his lifelong commitment to the revolution, a distinguished burial ceremony was prepared for him. The Palestinian flag was placed on his coffin. With great sadness, everyone in the funeral procession bid him farewell and accompanied his body to his last abode in the Christian cemetery Sulaibikhat. He was buried on a grey morning far away from Bogotá and Bethlehem that he had unreservedly loved.

Antonio's death pained me deeply. He left in me a heartbreak that time could never heal. My only consolation is that his deeds give him an eternal existence. His life will always be celebrated.

Antonio of Bethlehem

Epilogue

About the Author

Samih Masoud is a poet, writer, and researcher who was born in Haifa, Palestine in 1938. His elementary education at the al-Burj School of Haifa came to an abrupt end in third grade when his parents were forced to leave Haifa in 1948 for Burqa, where his family originally comes from. After completing his secondary education outside the Israeli-occupied Haifa, the author studied economics at the Sarajevo University, from where he has earned his Bachelor's Degree in 1963. He completed his Master's Degree at the Belgrade University in 1965, and earned his Ph.D. from the same university in 1967.

The author has served as an economic consultant for three regional Arabic establishments. In 1990, he was elected Chair to the Kuwaiti branch of the General Union for Palestinian Economists.

In addition to his published work in economics, including his two-volume *Encyclopedia of Economics* and nineteen additional books on his academic expertise, Samih Masoud has authored sixteen non-academic books, including *The Other Face of Days* – a collection of poems, and the documentary-memoirs, *Haifa . . . Burqa, A Search for Roots. Volume I*, *Haifa . . . Burqa, A Search for Roots. Volume II*, and *Haifa . . . Burqa, A Search for Roots. Volume III: A Memory of the Diaspora*. Many poems and scholarly articles of the author have been published in a large number of literary journals and newspapers.

The author is a member of the Jordanian Writers Association and the Arab Writers Union. He is the co-founder and Chair of the Canadian Center for Middle Eastern Studies (CMESC) in Montreal, Canada, and the General Secretary of the Al-Andalusi Cultural Center in the same Canadian city. This cultural center hosts gatherings for writers and publishes books in Arabic, English, and French.

Samih Masoud lives with his family in Montréal, Canada and in Amman, Jordan.

About the Translator

An avid writer and literary translator, Bassam S. Abu-Ghazalah was born in Nablus, Palestine and lives in Amman, Jordan. A member of The Jordanian Writers Society and The Arab Nationalist Congress, the majority of Dr. Abu-Ghazalah's writings –books of poetry, short stories and novels is composed in Arabic, the author's native tongue.

A pharmaceutist by profession with a degree in pharmacy from The American University of Beirut, Dr. Bassam S. Abu-Ghazalah has a prolific record of literary writings. His published offerings include *Rubaiyyat* – a book of poetry; *Across Jordan* – a novel; a multitude of short stories; books translated from English to Arabic, such as *Prelude to Israel* by Alan Tylor, *Confessions of an Economic Hit Man* by John Perkins, *Changing Venezuela by Taking Power* by Gregory Wilpert, *We Created Chavez* by George Ciccariello-Maher, and *Israel and the Clash of Civilizations* by Jonathan Cook; books translated from Arabic to English, such as the *Arab Social Life in Jerusalem in the 20th Century* by Subhi Ghosheh, *Haifa . . . Burqa, A Search for Roots. Volume I*, *Haifa . . . Burqa, A Search for Roots. Volume II* and *Haifa . . . Burqa, A Search for Roots. Volume III* by Samih Masoud, *al-Quds Is Not Jerusalem*, *The Fall of Jericho* and *The Myth of Crossing River Jordan* by Fadhel Rubayee.

The historical novel, *Bitter Love. An Image of the Palestinian Diaspora*, is the author's first book of prose in English.

Dr. Bassam S. Abu-Ghazalah lives in Amman, Jordan.

Other Books by the Author

The Roots of Andalusia (prose in Arabic).
Alaan Publishers: Amman, Jordan, 2020

Over the Steps of Clouds (poetry in Arabic).
Alaan Publishers: Amman, Jordan, 2020

Haifa . . . Burqa. A Search for Roots, Volume III: A Memory of the Diaspora (prose).
Translated by Bassam S. Abu-Ghazalah.
Inner Child Press International: USA, 2018

Haifa . . . Burqa. A Search for Roots, Volume II (prose).
Translated by Bassam S. Abu-Ghazalah
Inner Child Press International: USA, 2017

The Harvest of the Years.
Alaan Publishers: Amman, Jordan, 2017

Tatwan and Other Stories.
Alaan Publishers: Amman, Jordan, 2017

Haifa and Other Poems.
Translated into English by Nizar Sartawi
Inner Child Press International: USA, 2016

Haifa . . . Burqa. A Search for Roots. Volume I (prose).
Translated by Bassam S. Abu-Ghazalah.
Inner Child Press International: USA, 2016

Heritage Maqamat (a collection of art works).
Alaan Publishers: Amman, Jordan, 2015

The Museum of Haifa Memory. Family Collections from Haifa Before the Diaspora.
Alaan Publishers: Amman, Jordan, 2014

Visions and Contemplations (prose).
Fadaat Publishers: Amman, Jordan, 2013

The Other Face of Days (poetry).
Fadaat Publishers: Amman, Jordan, 2011

Inner Child Press

Inner Child Press is a publishing company founded and operated by writers. Our personal publishing experiences provide us an intimate understanding of the sometimes-daunting challenges writers, new and seasoned may face in the business of publishing and marketing their creative "Written Work".

For more information:

Inner Child Press

www.innerchildpress.com

intouch@innerchildpress.com

'building bridges of cultural understanding'

202 Wiltree Court, State College, Pennsylvania 16801

www.ingramcontent.com/pod-product-compliance
Lightning Source LLC
Chambersburg PA
CBHW070548160426
43199CB00014B/2416